THE

RISE

OF A

SOUL SOLDIER

Honoring Every Battle.
Lifting Every Soul

By

LINDSAY TAYLOR

To request permissions, contact the publisher
at publish@joapublishing.com

Hardcover ISBN: 978-1-961098-99-2
Paperback ISBN: 978-1-961098-98-5
eBook ISBN: 978-1-967575-00-8
Printed in the USA.

Joan of Arc Publishing
Meridian, ID 83646
www.joapublishing.com

✦ Enjoy Exclusive Bonuses! ✦

Thank you for reading The Rise of a Soul Soldier. As a special thank you, I've created exclusive bonuses just for you.

How to Access
Your Book Bonuses

Simply scan the QR code below with your phone to unlock your special resources:

iv

THE RISE OF A SOUL SOLDIER

THE

RISE

OF A

SOUL SOLDIER

vi

TABLE OF CONTENTS

Dedication xi

Acknowledgements xiii

A Heartfelt Message to My Reader xx

Part 1: My Cave **1**

Chapter 1: From Inside the Cave 2

Chapter 2: The Middle of the Cave 11

Chapter 3: The Depths of the Cave 19

Part 2: The Cave Begins to Turn **35**

Chapter 4: The Rainbow Beyond the Storm 36

Chapter 5: The Alchemy of Suffering: Turning Pain into Purpose 45

Chapter 6: Grieving with Grace 51

Chapter 7: Hope Beyond the Cave 59

Chapter 8: Unseen Warriors 66

Part 3: Exploring Your Cave **91**

Chapter 9: The Turn in Your Cave 92

Chapter 10: Miracle Mashers: Understanding the Patterns That Keep Us Stuck 99

Chapter 11: Miracle Masher #1: I Don't Belong 103

Chapter 12: Miracle Masher #2: I Am Not Worthy 116

Chapter 13: Miracle Masher #3: This Pain Will Never End 126

Part 4: The Exit from the Cave **137**

Chapter 14: Coming Home to Yourself..................................... 138

Chapter 15: From Death to Life 145

Chapter 16: Human Doing to Human Being 161

Chapter 17: The Ripple Effect 166

Chapter 18: The Sun Always Rises Again, and so Can YOU 171

Disclaimer

While this book is informed by my professional experience as a licensed therapist, it also draws upon personal stories and insights. It is not a substitute for clinical therapy or professional mental health treatment. The content shared here is intended to offer support, encouragement, and guidance, but it should not replace individualized care from a licensed mental health professional.

In instances where personal stories are shared, some names and identifying details have been changed to protect confidentiality, unless explicit consent was given.

If you are in crisis or in imminent danger, please seek immediate help. You are not alone. You can contact the **Suicide & Crisis Lifeline** by dialing **988**—support is available 24/7.

THE RISE OF A SOUL SOLDIER

x

DEDICATION

To every warrior who has walked the edge of darkness and found the courage to stay—you give the world hope. You give me the strength to keep returning to life's battlefield, to fight the good fight—the fight that saves and restores.

In loving memory of my son, my friend, my student, my brother, and all those who lost their fight too soon—your light lives on in the hearts of those who carry your memory. Your stories echo in every soul that rises in your honor.

To those who grieve a loved one lost to the battle with substance use or suicide—my heart is with you. May you find strength in knowing that love never dies.

To those who walk beside individuals in their darkest struggles—you are seen, you are valued, and your heart is needed in this world.

To every Soul Soldier standing in the fight for life—this is a call to rise, to reclaim your life. This is for all of us. We are not alone. We are united as warriors on this battleground called life.

And to you, the one holding this book—you are deeply loved, deeply seen. Your story is still being written. May these words remind you of your worth, your resilience, and the light that exists within you. No matter how dark the night, the dawn always comes.

With love and unwavering belief in your strength,

Lindsay

ACKNOWLEDGEMENTS

Bringing this book to life was a deeply emotional and life-changing journey. As I continue to show up in the world to help people reclaim and transform their lives, I find that my own life is continually changed in the process, and my soul expands in ways I never could have anticipated.

I could not have brought this book to life without God by my side, nor without the unwavering support of my mentor and business coach, Keira Brinton, and her incredible team at Joan of Arc Publishing. This book exists because of their dedication, and I am incredibly grateful for the entire JOA team.

To my friend and fellow leader, Brenda—your simple suggestion that I should write a book set everything in motion. That casual dinner conversation became the spark that set me on an adventure to write this book, which unfolded effortlessly without searching or trying. You have a heart of gold and I am forever grateful for your friendship, mentorship, and leadership in my life.

My heart is filled with admiration and love for everyone who has supported me on this journey. To those I have lost— my son, my friend, my student, my brother, and every soul who fought valiantly against addiction and suicidality—you are warriors. You fought battles that demanded unimaginable strength just to wake up and face another day. Your courage, even in the depths of your struggle, was extraordinary. You have touched my life and heart in ways that words can never fully capture—ways that have shaped me, broken me, and ultimately ignited an unshakable fire within me to help others find the light you fought so hard to hold on to.

Your lives mattered. Your struggles were not in vain. You have taught me what it truly means to fight—to fight for life, for hope, for the smallest flicker of light in the darkest of places. You have shown me the resilience of the human spirit and the heartbreaking reality of how heavy the fight can be.

Through this book, your stories will live on. They will reach hearts, spark hope, and remind those still in the fight that they are not alone. Your legacy is not one of loss, but of love—a love that continues to move through me, through these words, and through every life that finds healing because of the battles you fought. I honor you. I remember you. And I carry you with me, always.

To those who have entrusted me with your stories, allowing me to share them within these pages— thank you for your vulnerability, and willingness to share the rawest parts of your story. Your stories are powerful testaments to the resilience of the human spirit, the battles fought, and the triumph of choosing life even in the face of unbearable pain. You have shown me what resilience, hope, and faith look like in action.

I am humbled by your strength, inspired by your courage, and forever grateful that God wove our stories together. Your lives, your experiences, and your truths will reach others in ways you may never see, offering light to those still searching for their way through the darkness.

It is an honor to know you, to learn from you, and to walk alongside you in this journey called life. I hold your stories with deep reverence, and I promise, your voices will not fade; they will continue to echo in the hearts of those who need them most.

To my friends, my church family, my village—you are more than friends; you are the family my soul chose. Your unwavering support has been my anchor, your love a treasure. I am who I am because of the people who surround me, who pour into me, who believe in me. It is often said that *it takes a village,* and I am beyond grateful for the one I have.

To my bosses through the years and incredible coworkers—I have been truly blessed to work alongside such supportive and inspiring individuals. To my leaders and colleagues, thank you from the bottom of my heart for believing in me, seeing my potential, and uplifting me in ways that have shaped both my professional journey and my soul's calling. Stepping into leadership myself has been a humbling journey of growth, challenges, and learning. To my current team, thank you for your grace and willingness to grow alongside me and for also standing in the trenches to help save lives. I am deeply grateful for each of you. You make this world—and our workplace—a better place.

To my parents, my sister, my family—you have been my foundation, my safe harbor in life's storms, and the unwavering hands that have held me through it all. You have walked beside me, lifted me, and loved me unconditionally. In a world that often feels unsteady, you are my steady ground. Every lesson, every sacrifice, every moment of unwavering support has shaped me, fortified me, and given me the courage to step into my purpose. There are no words to express the depth of my gratitude. All I know is this—I am blessed beyond measure to call you family.

To the "little" humans who mean more to me than anything in this world—my children—you are my deepest source of love, strength, and purpose. You are the light that keeps me moving forward, the reason I rise each day with unwavering determination.

To my son Alex—my greatest teacher—you have taught me, and continue to teach me, what it means to be a mother in the truest sense. You pushed me to do my own healing, to look in the mirror and confront the patterns that no longer served me or those I love. Through you, my soul expanded in ways I never imagined, stretching me toward the person God intended me to be. Your presence graced me and this world with joy, and your absence is felt in every breath. Yet, I know your spirit is still here, woven into every rainbow and alive in every soul that finds hope within these pages. Your story, your love, your contagious smile and laugh will never fade. I thank God every day for you.

To my son Austin, my living example of grace. You have shown me, time and again, what unconditional love truly looks like. Through every mistake and shortcoming of mine, you have loved me still— without hesitation, without condition. You are a source of light and encouragement, a constant reminder of what true grace feels like. You are a special soul and this world is better off with you in it. You have a bright future ahead and I am so proud of you. God blessed me beyond measure when He gave me you.

To my daughter Arie, my reflection in the world. You walk this earth radiating a light so pure, a love so deep, and a heart so full of empathy—a heart this world desperately needs. Your presence is a gift to all who know you, and your love touches me in the gentlest, most beautiful way. Thank you for seeing me, for loving me so sweetly, and for reminding me of the softness in life. Keep shining that bright light of yours, baby girl. I am so proud of who you are and endlessly grateful that God gave me you.

To my daughter Ayla, my unexpected healing. The day you were born was the day I finally felt *good enough* as a mother. You reached into the deepest, most fragile parts of me—the place that longed for reassurance, that questioned her worth—and you filled that place with the purest love. Ever since that day, you have been my reminder that I am loved and that I am needed. And that is the greatest gift of all. You are a force to be reckoned with and the sweetest soul. You are going to move mountains, baby girl. You are a gift beyond words.

To my greatest supporter of all, the one I couldn't have done any of this without—my husband, my rock—you have stood beside me with unwavering love and support through life's highest highs and lowest lows. Our love story has been anything but ordinary—anything but easy—yet it is the greatest love I have ever known. A story of endurance, of choosing each other again and again, even when life tested us in ways we never saw coming.

You are my refuge, my soft place to land when the world feels too heavy. Your love is a testament to what it means to be steadfast—to show up, to hold on, to fight for something greater than the struggle itself. You are the home to my soul on this earth. God knew what He was doing when He brought us together. In you, He gave me a partner and a love that endures. For that, I am forever grateful.

ACKNOWLEDGEMENTS

A HEARTFELT MESSAGE TO MY READER

To the person opening the pages of this book: You are a miracle. Consider this: the odds of you being born, with your unique DNA, your story, your essence, are 1 in 400 trillion. Let that sink in. You are not an accident. You are not insignificant. You are a masterpiece created against all odds, a living, breathing miracle.

And yet, life doesn't always feel miraculous. At times, it can resemble a relentless and merciless battlefield—one fraught with pain, grief, and profound struggles. These struggles can overwhelm the mind, leading to a state of *dis-ease* that can manifest as diseases like depression, addiction, and other mental health challenges. Tragically, this dis-ease sometimes claims lives.

The battle with addiction and suicidal ideation (thoughts, ideas, or considerations about ending one's own life) is widespread. Every single one of us has either faced these battles personally, or we know someone who has, and many of us have tragically suffered losses to these battles. Every day, an average of 132 people die by suicide, and more than 130 Americans lose their lives to opioid-related overdoses. In his speech to the United States Congress, the country artist Jelly Roll put this statistic into perspective: this is equivalent to two full 737 passenger jets crashing every single day. Could you imagine? If such a tragedy were happening with airplanes, it would undoubtedly be deemed a national emergency. Yet, despite the alarming rise in suicide and drug-related deaths, these losses have quietly grown into a devastating epidemic.

The hopeful truth is that these tragedies are preventable. My deepest hope is that this book saves lives and ignites a collective movement to tackle the root causes that lead individuals into such dark and desperate places. If you or someone you love is struggling, know that I see you. Together, we can begin to turn the tide and rise as Soul Soldiers, reclaiming the light that exists in each of us and extending that light to a world that desperately needs it.

As a social worker and therapist, I've walked alongside individuals who are in excruciating pain—those battling addiction, suicidal ideation, immense grief, and overwhelming hardships. I've witnessed the struggles of people from all walks of life, from those who have endured homelessness and prison to those who are seemingly successful and appear to "have it all." Yet, one truth remains clear—struggle is universal. It knows no boundaries and finds its way into every life, regardless of circumstances. Having faced my own deep pain and tragedies, including the loss of my seventeen-year-old son to a fentanyl overdose, I've come to deeply understand the undeniable reality that struggle touches us all. No one is immune.

At the heart of suicidal ideation and addiction lies a pressing need to escape—a desperate search for relief. Over the past decade, I've observed recurring patterns in the struggles that often lead to escapism. These challenges, rooted in trauma and difficult life experiences, give rise to three core illusions:

1. **Belief that "I Don't Belong":** This illusion arises from the painful belief that one is alone, unseen, or unworthy of connection. When someone feels like they don't matter, that no one truly understands or cares, it can create a crushing sense of isolation. The absence of belonging or meaningful relationships leads to the illusion that they are disconnected from the world—when in truth, their presence matters more than they know, and connection is always possible, even if it hasn't been found yet.

2. **Belief that "I Am Not Enough":** This illusion is fueled by deep feelings of unworthiness, inadequacy, and sometimes shame. When someone believes they are broken, flawed, or fundamentally unlovable, they may begin to feel like a burden—convinced the world would be better off without them. This lack of self-worth blinds them to their inherent value and the truth that they are enough. That they are more than their mistakes, struggles, or past.

3. **Belief that "This Pain Will Never End":** This illusion is rooted in the belief that psychological pain is permanent and unbearable. When someone is overwhelmed by mental anguish, emotional distress, or deep internal suffering, it can feel as though there's no way out. They may underestimate their capacity to cope, not realizing that pain—no matter how intense—is often temporary and can be transformed with the right support, tools, and time.

This book delves into these deep illusions, which I call "miracle mashers," as they disconnect us from the miracles we truly are. In part three, I provide practical guidance for breaking free from the grip of these miracle mashers. The encouraging truth is that even amid this battlefield, hope remains. I've been humbled to witness extraordinary transformations—stories of people who have descended into the depths of despair, trapped by these illusions, yet found a way to rise from the darkness and reconnect with the truth of who they are.

Imagine a life where you feel worthy, where the pain and difficulties you face become manageable, and where you experience significance, belonging, and connection. These are fundamental human needs, and it is my hope that through these pages, you will discover the path to fulfilling them.

To those who battle addiction, suicidality, or the heavy weight of grief— the fight is as real and honorable as the struggles faced by soldiers on the frontlines. The enemies you confront are invisible but no less deadly—shame, despair, loneliness, and pain. You fight for your lives, your souls, and your futures. You bear wounds that may not bleed but cut just as deep. And just like soldiers, your resilience, will to survive, and courage make you heroes.

Overcoming these struggles is no less monumental than defeating cancer. Both battles demand strength, perseverance, and faith in something greater than the immediate pain. Both require a belief that life, however broken it may seem, is worth fighting for. Those who rise from these dark places are not merely survivors, they are warriors— Soul Soldiers—with scars that tell a story of resilience and rebirth. It is one of the most courageous battles anyone can fight. If this is you, I honor you in your fight.

The fight doesn't end with survival, though. It is in the aftermath, in the healing, that we find our purpose. Pain, as unbearable as it feels, can be a catalyst for vast growth. Our souls expand in ways that only hardship can teach us. *When the heart breaks, the soul learns to fly.*

In this space of expansion, we begin to see life not as something that happens *to* us but *for* us. Every trial, every heartache, and every moment of despair is part of a greater story—one beyond human comprehension. Call it God, the Universe, or Divine Love—whatever name you choose, there is a force greater than us, weaving meaning into our suffering, if we open our hearts to it.

And what about the inherent good in each of us? It's easy, in the throes of struggle, to lose sight of our worth. It's easy to feel unworthy of redemption, life change, or love. But no human life is beyond saving. No soul is beyond transformation. We are all capable of rising, no matter how far we've fallen. Each of us carries within us a spark of the Divine—a light that cannot be extinguished no matter how dark the night.

Whether you're in the middle of your own battle, climbing your way out, standing alongside a loved one who is struggling, or facing the immense grief that accompanies these battles, you have come to the right place—a place I hope you feel deeply seen and loved.

The struggles we face can feel like being lost in the depths of a dark cave, unable to see the light or find a way out. But here's the hopeful truth: no matter how deep in the cave you or your loved one is, there is a way out. This book is here to help illuminate that path.

Within these pages, I'll share my own personal tragedies and how falling to my knees in the depths of darkness became the beginning of my greatest rise toward the light. You'll also find stories of others who have transformed their pain into purpose, along with practical guidance to help you navigate your own cave and emerge stronger.

The book is divided into four parts for a seamless journey of reflection and transformation.

Part One (My Cave) delves into the depths of my own cave—one filled with grief and pain.

Part Two (The Cave Begins to Turn) explores how the cave begins to turn. This is not just a story of struggle; it's a story of survival and transformation. Through my darkest moments, I discovered that pain could become purpose, and that even in the deepest shadows, there is a way to rise. I weave together with my experiences the powerful stories of others who have faced the crushing pain of addiction, suicidal ideation, or both and emerged on the other side with hope, redemption, and life-changing transformation.

Part Three (Exploring Your Cave) invites you to step into your own cave. Here, you'll uncover the three Miracle Mashers (illusions and lies) that keep us from healing. Through guided journal prompts and self-reflection, you'll have the space to confront your own struggles and begin moving toward the light that heals.

Part Four (The Exit From The Cave) is a guide out of the cave and offers tools for hope, healing, and continued growth. This final section provides opportunities for reflection, helping you embrace the miracle you are as you move forward.

Wherever you are, whatever you are facing, I hope through these pages that you will come to see that you are not alone in this fight. You are loved deeply. Your story matters. Your pain has a purpose. You are a Soul Soldier, and this world needs the light only you can bring.

I invite you to walk this journey with me. Together, we will rise.

PART 1

MY CAVE

Chapter 1

FROM INSIDE
THE CAVE

Theodore Roosevelt is credited with saying, "People don't care how much you know until they know how much you care." These words resonate deeply with me because the moments that have helped me most weren't just about knowledge, they came from hearing the stories of others—stories of pain, tragedy, and suffering—and their journeys out of the darkness toward hope, healing, and redemption.

These stories do more than offer understanding—they instill hope. Hearing how someone climbed out of their cave of despair breathes life into us. It reminds us that survival and healing are possible. That's why stories like this are woven throughout the pages of this book—because they reach our hearts and touch our souls, the true places where healing takes place.

I want to take a moment here to acknowledge this: you'll find God woven throughout these pages, because God has been essential in not only my healing journey but also the journeys of others I will share about. His guidance helped bring this book to life. But this book is not about religion. It's about grace, love, and the deeply personal journey of each soul.

I know that even hearing (or reading) the word "God" can bring up resistance for some. If this is where you are, I see you, and I deeply understand. As a child, I attended a Lutheran church with my family, but in my teenage years, I stepped away. I felt that God was so much bigger than any one religion, including Christianity. I didn't believe in a single "right" way to connect with God, and over time, I became more spiritual than religious. And for over a decade, I didn't have much of a relationship with God at all.

Then, just before I walked into the darkest chapter of my life, God reached me in a way I couldn't ignore. By His grace, I found my way back—not to religion, but to a relationship. Even so, I carried resistance. I was deeply resistant to return to church. But God had other plans—plans that would change the trajectory of my grief in a way that ultimately saved me on this deeply painful journey.

I did find my way back to church. I found a church that embraced me exactly as I was—doubts, imperfections, questions, and all. It's a church whose motto resonated deeply with me: "No matter where you've been, what you've done, or what's been done to you, you belong here." This church even has a prison ministry that brings hope to those behind bars, which is deeply important to me. Through this church, I've been able to grow closer to God again.

For a long time, I resisted Jesus because I equated Him solely with Christianity as a religion. I realized a relationship with Jesus, and the love and light that Jesus brings to this world, exists outside of religion. Today, I attend a Christian church, but I still struggle with the belief that Christianity is the "one and only way." What I do believe in—and what has transformed me—is God's love, His grace, His redemption, and His light. That is what we all need. Jesus saves and restores, and I have witnessed this truth time and time again in my own life and the lives of others.

I honor you, wherever you are on your spiritual journey. I welcome all backgrounds, all belief systems, and all stories. My hope is simply that, in whatever way feels true to you, you come to find that there is something greater at work in this world and in your life, bringing peace and hope.

Hope—the other key element of this book—I've learned, is essential to overcoming life's difficulties. In this book, I'll weave together the threads of my personal and professional experiences, sharing insights and stories that have shaped my understanding of addiction, suicidality, profound grief, and the human capacity for resilience. Together, we'll explore the caves of my own life and the lives of others, discovering how the cave turns, ultimately providing light and hope for your journey.

The first time I found myself personally in the depths of a cave was in 2008. I was consumed by debilitating anxiety. I could barely leave my house. I was diagnosed with agoraphobia and panic disorder. The panic attacks were relentless, suffocating me in a prison of fear. At my lowest point, I was the closest I ever got to thoughts of suicide. I remember sitting in despair and thinking, *I can't live the rest of my life feeling like this.* It was a dark and isolating time.

I stayed in the fight, one day at a time. I fought hard to retrain my brain and reclaim my life. Therapy was a catalyst, but one book in particular, *Anxiety Free* by Robert Leahy, was life-changing. It set the stage for my recovery, offering practical tools to face my fears and build resilience. Over time, with consistent effort and a willingness to confront the discomfort, the grip of anxiety began to loosen. It was a lonely and difficult road, one that took a couple years to walk, but as I stayed in the fight and walked the path, I discovered how the cave turned and I began to see the light again. Today, aside from "typical anxiety" that creeps in from time to time, I can truly say I am anxiety-free, and I credit Leahy's book as the pivotal turning point in my journey. Books can be life-changing, and I hope through this book you can get your life back like I did mine.

The first time I found myself sitting in the depths of someone else's cave was in 2015. It was a cool winter night when I received a phone call. A mutual friend told me that our close friend Zach (whose name I've changed for privacy) was in crisis—suicidal, on the brink of taking his life. Our mutual friend couldn't go to Zach that night and asked me to step in.

When I arrived at Zach's house, I instantly felt how serious the situation was. It was my first time sitting in the deepest abyss of darkness with someone who was suicidal, and I felt the weight and thickness of it. I could feel the smothering of the blanket that was around us. It felt suffocating. It felt dark. It felt scary. *I* was afraid. I can only imagine how Zach felt. There was alcohol involved, and so there was some unpredictability to what Zach was going to do in those moments as I tried to get him to come with me. He was resistant at first, saying he didn't need help. I tried my best to just hold space for Zach, to sit with him in his immense pain and let him know he was not alone. I tried to bring a little light to a very dark night in hopes of helping him stay in the battle, to come with me and choose to continue to live. I had no idea what I was doing. Being there and sitting with him was all I knew to do. His emotions were all over the place, so I just held space and rode the wave of emotions with him. Eventually, Zach got to a state of mind where he was able to calm down enough to get in my car, and he agreed to come with me.

That night, amid his suffering, Zach chose life. He would spend the next couple of years working on himself and fighting for his life. People who are suicidal are fighters. They battle, just like those battling cancer and fighting to live. It takes special strength to carry on and see another day when you are battling thoughts of suicide. It takes immense courage and strength to choose life when darkness has taken hold. For Zach, this was a battle he fought for many years while going in and out of sobriety. After that night, he found himself yet again picking up the pieces and continuing to fight for his life. Zach got sober and began to do well for the next few years. He ended up meeting a girl and falling in love.

In 2017, Zach married the love of his life. It was a sunny, winter day in the beautiful foothills of Colorado. As the ceremony began, I remember sitting in the crowd and just feeling such joy as I watched Zach—beaming with pride and full of life—stand in front of his bride. To go from sitting with him on his darkest day to now bearing witness to the light that radiated around him on the best day of his life touched my heart beyond what words can articulate. I wanted nothing more than the best for Zach. Watching someone we love and care about become unrecognizable due to their struggles is devastating, and losing them permanently is our greatest fear, so being able to see them alive and thriving touches the heart in the most indescribable way.

Later that evening, a beautiful reception brought everyone together. Zach stood up to speak, addressing each guest with heartfelt words. He shared that he had been very intentional about whom he invited, ensuring that everyone present held a special place in his heart.

When he reached me, he paused, gathering his emotions. With deep gratitude, he thanked me for being there that night a few years prior and for "saving him." He shared that he wouldn't be alive, wouldn't have made it to this moment—his wedding day, the best day of his life—without me. It humbled me and filled me with joy to see him standing there so full of life.

It's important to develop an understanding that, while I supported Zach and helped him through that night, his survival was ultimately due to *him choosing life that night*. When it comes to helping someone who is suicidal, their life is not in anyone else's hands but their own. We can be there for them, offering support and care, which can make all the difference, as it did with Zach, but the choice of what happens next is ultimately theirs.

If you're supporting someone who is suicidal or struggling with substance use, remember that their life does not rest on your shoulders. This is a reality that is far beyond your control. Over the years, both in my personal and professional life, being so close to those battling suicidal ideation and addiction, I've learned this truth: while your support can be life-changing, their journey and choices remain their own.

After Zach got married in 2017, I was living in Arizona while Zach was in Colorado. We would occasionally text each other, but we didn't stay in regular contact. Then, on December 4, 2018, I was on my way to a massage appointment when I suddenly felt an intense rush—almost like a gust of wind and chills—move through my body. It was completely out of the blue and rather overwhelming. Right after, a thought came to me: *I wonder how Zach is doing*. I realized it had been a while since we'd last talked, and the urge to check on him was strong.

As I exited the highway, a thought came to me that I should look him up on Facebook when I got to the next stoplight, to see if he had posted anything recently. Upon checking, I saw there were no recent posts. When the light turned green, I thought, *I need to text him*. But I was running late for my appointment and thought, *I'll text him as soon as I'm done*. Unfortunately, after my appointment, I forgot to send him a message.

The next morning, while I was in the bathroom getting ready, my husband walked in with a concerned look on his face. Then, the words I had been fearing came out of his mouth. In a somber tone, he said, "Did you hear that Zach passed away?" Those words hit me like a punch to the gut. My heart sank, and I stood there in stunned silence.

My mind immediately flashed back to the day before, realizing I had forgotten to text Zach. A wave of emotions surged as I shared that story with my husband. Then came the flood of "what ifs." What if I had reached out? Would it have made a difference? Would he still be alive?

I ultimately knew it wasn't in my control and dwelling on the "what ifs" wouldn't change anything, but my mind kept returning to

2015 when Zach had been in crisis, and I had been able to help. *What if* I could have done that again? The emotions were overwhelming as I struggled to process and make sense of it all.

At that point, all we knew was that Zach had passed away. To make matters more difficult, I was three days away from giving birth, and unfortunately the funeral was a week after my daughter was born, so I was unable to make it to the funeral. It was a heartbreaking reality layered with unanswered questions and grief.

The cause of Zach's death was never publicly announced, but it became known that he died by suicide. For years, the uncertainty surrounding his passing weighed heavily on me. I eventually shared on Zach's Facebook tribute wall a brief version of the story of the day I felt I needed to reach out to Zach but forgot to. I couldn't stop wondering if that rush of energy I'd felt on December 4th was Zach reaching out from the other side or if he had still been alive at that moment.

His wife later commented on my post, letting me know that he had passed away early in the morning on December 3rd. Her response brought a sense of closure, and I realized that the rush I felt was Zach's presence with me from the other side, a comforting reality we'll explore through this book.

Although Zach sadly lost his battle to suicide, his story offers hope that it is possible to rise from the darkest of places and find life again. Zach would have never experienced the love he did and the best day of this life had it ended sooner. In the same breath, Zach's story also highlights the tragic reality that one can be pulled back into that darkness. Sadly, some do lose their battle, whether it's with suicidality, addiction, cancer, or other struggles.

Loss is an inevitable part of life, and while we may never fully understand why some recover and others do not, I have come to a deep inner knowing that there is a higher purpose woven into all of our lives and stories. Through the pages of this book, you will come to see this truth and find hope, even in the midst of the deepest tragedies and hardest-fought battles.

Chapter 2

THE MIDDLE OF THE CAVE

Professionally, my journey has brought me into the lives of individuals facing immense struggles. From 2016 to 2018, I worked at an adoption agency as a case manager working with birth mothers placing a child for adoption. Many of these mothers were making this selfless yet heartbreaking decision while battling addiction. Once again, I found myself walking alongside people in the darkest moments of their lives, striving to bring a glimmer of hope to the shadows that consumed them. That job became deeply meaningful to me and will always hold a special place in my heart.

During that time, I gained a profound understanding of the power of addiction. I witnessed up close the immense love these mothers and fathers had for their babies and how deeply it tore them apart to selflessly place their child in another family's hands. Yet, I also saw how overpowering addiction was. The love for your child is one of the strongest forces imaginable, but even that love, as deep and unconditional as it is, can often be overcome by the insurmountable stronghold of addiction. It was a sobering and heartbreaking realization of just how insidious and consuming addiction can be.

One mother I worked with, who battled both addiction and suicidality, shared that one day when I showed up to her door, she was on the verge of taking her life. She later told me I saved her life that day. The truth is, this is so much bigger than me. First, *she* chose life that day, as *she* made the decision to answer the door and come with me. Secondly, in hindsight, I realize each place and situation I have found myself in, helping someone in their darkest hour, both knowingly and unknowingly, has been divine intervention—God placing me in the right place at the right moment. I'm just a vessel, a part of His army, here to bring love and light to places where it's been lost.

In 2019, I transitioned into a new role as a high school social worker, supporting the social, emotional, and mental health needs of students. It was in this position that I began working more frequently with individuals battling suicidality. One student, whom I'll refer to as Ty, left a particularly deep imprint on my heart.

I first met Ty in the fall of 2020, shortly after he returned to school following a suicide attempt. When we met, he was withdrawn, keeping his head down and avoiding eye contact. Over the following months, we developed a rapport as I met with him regularly. I'll never forget the day he lifted his head and looked at me as we talked. It felt like a small yet meaningful breakthrough. His pain was palpable, and I wanted so badly to help him through it.

In early 2021, Ty attempted suicide again. When he returned to school, he came into my office, handed me his phone, and said, "I want you to read this." On his phone was a journal entry he had written processing his struggles with suicidality. As I scrolled through his words, it was the first time I could see and feel into the suicidal mind. His pain radiated from the screen, so raw and overwhelming that it was as if I were standing in the middle of his cave, surrounded by his despair.

Together, we began to process what he had written, unpacking the weight of his words. He indicated that the intent behind what he had written was to just process his feelings, but he was not actively suicidal or in danger.

That night, I went home and sobbed as I processed what Ty had shared. At times, it can be hard not to carry the weight of the struggles of those I help because this work is my soul's work, and I care immensely. I felt like I had the weight of his world resting on my shoulders, and I desperately wanted to help him in every way I could. Yet, I also felt the weight of knowing that his needs extended far beyond what I could offer in my role or with my skill set at the time. Still, I poured all that I had into supporting him the best I could.

Over the next couple of months, Ty improved. Just before the end of April, I experienced something that, in hindsight, was undeniably divine—that moment I spoke about in the first chapter when God showed up in a way that couldn't be ignored. It was an ordinary afternoon at the gym, and I was training with my coach when the conversation unexpectedly shifted to spirituality. This was completely out of character for him; he wasn't someone who typically talked about faith. But that day, he did.

He told me about an Alpha group he had recently joined, and he quite adamantly encouraged me to try it out. For those unfamiliar, Alpha is a group designed for atheists, agnostics, and those questioning their faith or not sure where they stand spiritually. It's a space to explore life's biggest questions, learn about Jesus, and grow in faith without pressure or judgment. As I mentioned earlier, I had grown up going to church and had always believed in God, but I had drifted away in my teenage years. While I still considered myself spiritual, I had long struggled with my stance on organized religion.

At first, I wasn't sure if Alpha was something I wanted to explore. But after a few conversations and a strong nudge from my coach, I decided to give it a try. I had no idea that this decision would lead me back to a relationship with God in a way I never expected. While I firmly believe you don't need organized religion to have a relationship with God, for me, finding a church that was welcoming and accepting of ALL people, became a pivotal moment—one that would shape how I navigated the devastating turn my life was about to take.

On Thursday, April 29, 2021—a week after joining Alpha—I had another experience that, looking back, felt undeniably divine. It came through an unexpected conversation with my intern—one that would once again change the trajectory of the darkest, most difficult chapter I was about to enter.

That day, she opened up about a recent experience with a psychic medium. She shared how impactful it was in processing the loss of a close friend years earlier. Knowing about Zach and the many unanswered questions surrounding his passing, she strongly encouraged me to meet with this medium.

At first, I was hesitant. I wasn't sure how I felt about psychics or mediums, and it wasn't something I'd ever considered pursuing. But as we talked, I felt a sudden shift inside me—a strong, undeniable nudge that said, *You need to do this.* Almost without thinking, I said, "Okay, I'm going to text him right now and book an appointment." Immediately, I reached out and scheduled a session for the following Wednesday, May 5, 2021.

At the time, I had no clue how significant those moments were. But shortly thereafter, it became apparent that they were divine breadcrumbs guiding me toward something greater, preparing me for what was to come.

On Sunday morning, at the beginning of May, I was driving when a call came through from my boss. She never called on Sundays, so I immediately knew it must be serious. I answered, and her tone confirmed my fears.

"Lindsay, are you by yourself?" she asked.

"Yes," I replied.

"Are you in a place where I can share something with you?"

"Yes," I said again, bracing myself for what was coming.

Her next words hit me like a ton of bricks. "Ty is in the hospital. He attempted suicide, and it's not looking good. He is likely going to pass away." A short while later, he passed.

My heart sank. I felt crushed, utterly devastated by the loss of Ty to this battle. Another warrior, another fighter, another beautiful soul taken too soon. There are no words to capture the weight of such a tragedy. It was shattering in every sense.

As I tried to process what had happened, my mind turned to the appointment I had scheduled to meet with the psychic medium just a few days later. The timing of that session would prove to be nothing short of astonishing—something that only God could orchestrate so perfectly to reach me in the depths of my grief as the week unfolded.

During my appointment with the psychic medium, he shared several mind-blowing insights that left me speechless. To preface, when I booked the session, the only information he received was my first name and the email address to send the Zoom link to. He knew nothing else about me, yet the things he said were instantly specific and deeply personal.

Almost immediately, he brought up Ty, and not long after, Zach. At one point, he said, "They keep saying 'suicide.' Are you going to specialize in suicide?" The question caught me off guard. My first thought was, *Specialize? Is that even a specialty?*

I replied, "I work with teens who are struggling with thoughts of suicide, and I've been impacted personally. But specialize?" I had never even considered that, let alone imagined it being my specialty. Looking back, it's incredible to realize how that moment marked the beginning of what would become my future path—a journey that feels, yet again, divinely paved.

He then said, "They're saying three, like maybe it's going to come in threes." Those words sent a chill through me. My mind immediately went to my son Alex as we were facing a particularly challenging situation with him at the time. I tried to dismiss the fear, but it lingered in the back of my mind.

The psychic medium then asked, "What's the deal with the rainbow?" Unsure, I replied, "I don't know." He pressed further, "What does a rainbow mean to you?" I said, "Hope." He nodded and said, "Okay, there's something with a rainbow. You need to pay attention to that."

Toward the end of the session, he mentioned the rainbow again, saying, "There's something really strong with a rainbow. Pay attention to it." I ended the call and immediately told my husband about the session. My husband, a complete skeptic, was hesitant to believe any of it, but he agreed to listen to the recording. I shared my growing concern about Alex based on what the psychic medium had said. My husband tried to reassure me with his skepticism, saying, "No, it will be okay. Nothing is going to happen." While I wanted to cling to this belief, the fear lingered.

At the end of that difficult week, on Saturday, I attended Ty's memorial. My boss, who lived near the park where the memorial was held, invited me to meet at her house to go to the memorial together. That evening, as I left her house, the weight of grief felt almost unbearable. I carried not only my own grief but also the grief of Ty's friends, classmates, and family, all devastated by his loss.

Sensing how heavy the week had been for me, my boss offered me some advice as I prepared for the next day, which happened to be Mother's Day. She said, "Lindsay, set this aside tomorrow. Be fully present with your family and kids. They need you. Don't think about work—just focus on enjoying your family."

Her words were exactly what I needed to hear. That reminder to be present with my children, to pour love into them, was grounding for me. The reality that *tomorrow is not guaranteed* was closing in on me, and I knew how important it was to treasure each moment with my family.

Chapter 3

THE DEPTHS OF
THE CAVE

I went home that night after Ty's memorial, ready to enjoy time with my family. My sister had come into town for Mother's Day weekend, and that evening, she, her boyfriend, my husband, and I decided to spend a night out together. We went to dinner and then headed to a local bar that had a patio—a fun spot where we could sit back, relax, and enjoy each other's company. It was exactly what I needed after such a long and emotional week.

The evening was going well. We were all enjoying ourselves when, just after midnight, my husband's phone started ringing. He glanced at the screen and said, "It's a Phoenix number. I wonder if I should answer it." Something about the timing felt strange to both of us, and after exchanging a quick look, we agreed he should pick up.

My first thought was that it might be law enforcement; I assumed Alex had gotten himself into trouble because of some of the decisions he'd been making. But as soon as my husband answered the call and said, "Hello," I saw the look of horror take over his face. His mouth dropped open, he grabbed his head, and darted out of the bar.

Everything happened so fast. My brain was struggling to process what was going on, but the expression on his face told me something was seriously wrong.

My heart sank, and a thought came to my mind: *Alex died.*

I sat there, frozen in silence. Noticing the obvious distress, my sister had the same initial thought I had. Worriedly, she asked "Do you think Alex is in jail?"

"No," I said in shock, "I think he's dead."

Her eyes widened in panic. "Are you going to go help Matt!?!"

Her words jolted me into action. Adrenaline kicked in, and I bolted from the table. Outside, I found my husband on his knees in the gravel, still on the phone. I rushed toward him and dropped beside him, asking, "Is he dead? Is he dead?" My husband held up his hand, signaling for me to wait.

When he finally hung up, he turned to me, his face distraught with shock. "That was the charge nurse at Chandler Regional," he said, his voice trembling. "Alex's friends brought him to the hospital and he had no pulse. The staff worked on him for sixteen minutes and were able to get his heart restarted, but it's not looking good. We need to get there fast."

Disbelief consumed me. I couldn't wrap my mind around what was happening, but I knew I had to pull myself together and go into action. Our car was parked quite a distance from the bar, so I urgently began looking for a way to get to it quickly. By now, people around us could see we were in crisis. A man on a taxi bike approached and asked, "Do you guys need a ride?"

"Yes, please," I responded urgently.

By that point, my sister and her boyfriend had come outside after quickly settling the bill, and we all hurried to the parking garage.

You don't realize how many emotions you can experience at once until you're faced with a tragedy of this magnitude. I felt shocked, angry, sad, confused, worried—and somewhere deep inside, faintly hopeful. On the surface, I forced myself to remain composed, knowing I had to hold it together to get us to the hospital.

As we drove, my husband, incredibly distraught, kept repeating, "I think he's dead. I just know he's dead."

Trying to steady him and myself, I said, "Let's just hold on to hope and wait until we talk to the charge nurse."

When we arrived at the hospital, we were quickly taken back to a room. My mind was racing, the same thoughts looping over and over: *Is this really happening? Am I dreaming? Is this some kind of nightmare? This can't be real.*

We sat in silence, tense and anxious, until the door opened and in came the charge nurse. He sat down next to us, his demeanor gentle and empathetic. In a soft voice, he began to explain what had happened and Alex's condition.

He told us that Alex's friends, who we had seen standing outside when we arrived, had driven him to the hospital. When they arrived, Alex had no pulse. A police officer had come to speak with the friends, as details about what happened before they brought him in were still unclear. They had reported that Alex had taken fentanyl and that they had found him unconscious at a park, which we later found out was a lie. (I will share more about what happened that night in Part 4 when we explore forgiveness.)

The nurse explained that the medical team was able to resuscitate Alex after sixteen minutes, but they didn't know how long he had gone without oxygen before that. He told us Alex was now on a ventilator and in critical condition.

Since Alex was seventeen, the nurse said they would need to airlift him to the children's hospital once he was stable enough for transport. I remember the nurse looking at us after telling us what had happened and saying, "I'm so sorry." We deeply felt his kindness in that moment. He asked if we had any questions, and we took a moment to ask a few. Then, he described what we could expect when we entered Alex's room and gently asked if we were ready to see him.

As he led us to Alex's room, I felt a wave of overwhelming anxiety settle in. I wasn't sure what we were about to walk into.

When we arrived at Alex's room, I was immediately overcome with emotion. Tears streamed down my face as I watched the nurses working around him, suctioning his lungs. They explained that he had aspirated a significant amount.

The sight was overwhelming—Alex was connected to countless machines, tubes seemingly everywhere. It felt like a living nightmare. My mind continued to race with questions and disbelief: *How did we get here? How could this be happening?* Never in a million years did I imagine this would be our reality.

I just wept beside him, and all I could do was whisper, "I'm so sorry," over and over again. My heart shattered as I looked at him; I was consumed by sadness that this is where things ended up. Through the tears, I kept repeating, "I'm sorry" and "I love you, Buddy."

Let me tell you about Alex. When Alex was just one year old, and I was the ripe age of sixteen, I began taking care of him as his babysitter. Life took a wild and unexpected turn when Alex's mom and dad separated two years later. Shortly thereafter, his dad and I, in a natural and organic way, came together and fell in love. Alex's brother, our son Austin, was a newborn when the boys' dad and I began dating. I found myself at eighteen years old jumping in and helping to love them, care for them, and raise them as my own alongside their Dad.

Alex had the sweetest, most sensitive soul. He was a national-level competitive gymnast from the ages of seven to sixteen. Gymnastics was his passion and meant the world to him for many years. Over time, he earned countless medals and accolades for his incredible talent.

After stepping away from gymnastics, Alex's love for skateboarding grew and quickly became a new passion. A naturally gifted athlete, he excelled at any sport or activity he tried.

Alex was a social kid. He loved spending time with his friends and seeking out new adventures. He was known for his radiant smile that could light up any room, his contagious laugh, and his caring soul.

Sadly, beneath Alex's radiant smile and sweet nature, he carried a deep struggle: he was affected by the absence of his biological mom in his life. Also, when he quit gymnastics, he lost a significant part of his identity. Gymnastics had defined him for so long that without it, he didn't know who he was. These internal battles eventually caught up to him.

Things took a drastic turn when the COVID-19 pandemic hit in March of 2020. Alex began heavily using marijuana, which triggered a rapid and devastating decline. We watched our healthy, happy, vibrant teen transform into someone we hardly recognized—a young boy struggling intensely with his mental health.

Although Alex faced struggles throughout his childhood due to the absence of his mom, he had never been a depressed or anxious child. He had always been active and social. But here he was, in a state of mind of increasingly more fragile mental health. He eventually developed marijuana-induced psychosis. I always say we lost Alex to the marijuana first.

While it was fentanyl that ultimately stopped his heart, it was marijuana that set Alex on a destructive path—one that damaged his mind and eventually cost him his life. I learned just how harmful marijuana can be for a developing brain, especially when used in excess.

I want to take a moment here and speak directly to those who have a child battling substance use or suicidal thoughts—the pain is unlike anything else. As parents, our greatest desire is to protect our children and see them happy and thriving. But when confronted with the stark reality of their deep struggles and the realization that we cannot "fix" it for them, the devastation feels insurmountable.

I remember the summer of 2020 when things had taken a devastating turn with Alex. One day, the weight of it all became unbearable, leaving me physically ill from the anguish. As I sat there, consumed by despair, it hit me—this was far bigger than anything I could handle or fix on my own. I knew I had to lean on God. So, in my desperation, I prayed—to a God I had barely spoken to in a long time. In that moment of raw vulnerability, I felt God speak life-giving words into my soul that changed everything: "You must turn inward and surrender."

It was a moment of profound clarity, like lightning striking my heart. I realized the only thing I had control over was myself—not Alex's choices, not the outcome of his struggle—just me and my actions and reactions. As parents, we often have this false sense that we can *control* what our kids do and who they become. I have learned that *we certainly have influence.* So when I say I surrendered, I didn't give up on trying to have a relationship with him that was centered on love while also putting appropriate boundaries and rules in place and striving to influence him in a positive direction. But I knew I could not "control him" or "change" him. He had to be the one to do that for himself. He was his *own human.* Our kids are their own people.

This leads me to another trap I realized we as parents can fall into, and that is internalizing our kids' actions or struggles, thinking it's a direct reflection on us. Again, we have influence—something I intimately understand—but our kids' choices and actions are ultimately their own. I realized I had to focus on loving Alex first (leading with love) while putting boundaries in place, and then leave the rest up to him. Therefore, my mindset and actions shifted from "control" to focusing on influence. Then, I made a commitment to focus on what I *could* control—how I was showing up and behaving—and then surrender what was beyond my control. It was both the hardest and most liberating decision I've ever made.

I chose to support Alex, to stand by him in love, but not allow his pain to destroy my peace. From that moment on, an unshakable calm settled within me—a peace that sustained me even as we faced unimaginable heartbreak. That moment of surrender didn't change the external challenges, and I still faced the deep emotions surrounding our situation, but it transformed me. It prepared me for the tragedy that would follow and gave me the strength to endure.

Turning inward and focusing on what is within your control is key to supporting someone struggling with addiction or suicidal ideation. It doesn't mean ignoring their pain or stepping away from them; it means protecting your inner peace and focusing on the influence you have while setting boundaries and finding the strength within yourself to face the storm with love and resilience. Setting healthy boundaries and focusing on what is within your control allows you to be a steady, loving presence without losing yourself in their struggle. It's important to avoid the trap of enabling, which only prolongs the problem. The key is to let them know you're there for them when they're ready to seek help while maintaining clear boundaries and allowing them the space to take that step on their own. If your child is a minor, "forced" treatment may very well be the answer. In our case, we felt it would only make things worse, and so we compromised with the help Alex was willing to receive.

In the last eight months of Alex's life, things became rocky. He began running away, and eventually, he moved in with a friend. This shift only deepened his decline. By December 2020, Alex began experiencing suicidal thoughts and even asked to be hospitalized. This was shocking, as just a year earlier, Alex had strong opinions against suicide and couldn't comprehend why anyone would take their own life. I had once explained it to him from a place of compassion, helping him understand the immense pain and agony someone is in to reach that point. I told him that those battling thoughts of suicide are far from selfish. They are warriors, full of strength, fighting an unimaginable battle.

Then, Alex found himself in the very place he thought he'd never be: deep in a cave, fighting for his life. After his hospitalization in 2020, we believed Alex needed residential treatment, but he was deeply resistant. He did agree, however, to weekly counseling and sessions with a psychiatrist. So, we did our best to support him, navigating his reluctance and working tirelessly to get him the help he needed.

In March of 2021, Alex confided in my husband that he had tried fentanyl, fully aware it could kill him. Once again, he found himself battling to live. Following this admission, he was hospitalized for the second time.

By then, we knew we had to get him into treatment, whether he agreed or not. Desperate for a solution, we reached out to his mom (who lived out of state) to see if Alex could stay with her. The plan was for him to finish high school while living with her. He was a senior and we needed time to arrange for a treatment facility. She agreed, and Alex was happy about the arrangement because he hadn't seen his mom in many years.

During his five weeks with his mom, Alex completed his classes online and expressed a strong desire to come home for his graduation, which was set for mid-May. He was eager to return, and we had a treatment center ready for him upon his return. However, Alex insisted he attend his graduation first before entering treatment. Despite our hesitation, we ultimately agreed.

When Alex came back from his mom's, he refused to stay at our house and was adamant about returning to his friend's place. We strongly discouraged it, but once again, we found ourselves at a crossroads. We had reached a point where we couldn't force him to stay home. Feeling powerless, we focused on what we could control—being a loving presence and setting healthy boundaries—while managing the situation as best we could. All the while, we hoped and prayed he would make it through this difficult period and eventually find his way out of the cave.

We were deeply concerned but chose to hope that he would make it to his graduation. From there, we planned to move forward with treatment, hoping it would provide the help he desperately needed.

Alex flew home on May 5, 2021, the same day I had an appointment with the psychic medium. I was filled with anxiety about his return, knowing he would be staying at his friend's house, an environment that wasn't healthy for him. The thought of it weighed heavily on me, adding to the immense grief I was already carrying that week following the loss of my student.

By that Friday, I was completely overwhelmed—emotionally, mentally, and physically. I remember sitting down with a coworker and feeling utterly exhausted. I shared with her that Alex had come home, but I couldn't let myself think about it too much because it made me sick with worry knowing where he was staying. At that point, I was just trying to survive the week, navigating the whirlwind of emotions I was already dealing with.

I told her my plan was to get through Ty's memorial service the next day and then see Alex on Sunday for Mother's Day. I was holding on to that, looking forward to spending time with him after such a difficult and draining week.

And now, here I was at 1:00 a.m. on Mothers Day (May 9, 2021), coming off of a significant loss and a very emotional week, standing next to Alex's hospital bed with this gut-wrenching realization that I might be facing the most devastating heartbreak and loss yet.

As Alex lay there unconscious, hooked up to the breathing machine and hardly recognizable, I was grief-stricken. Shock and disbelief continued to consume me. My heart was breaking into a million pieces seeing him for the first time in two months, in that condition. With tears flowing down my cheeks while I whispered, "I'm so sorry, Buddy. I'm so sorry," my mind raced with desperate thoughts of what I wouldn't give to have him back, to see him healthy and happy again.

But instead, we were in the middle of a dire situation, lost in the depths of a dark and suffocating cave, teetering on the verge of losing our son.

Alex was airlifted to the local children's hospital. When we arrived, the ICU doctor met us in the waiting room to provide an update. He explained that they were working to stabilize Alex but said, "It's not looking good. We're going to do everything we can to help him, but we need to test for brain activity to determine if recovery is possible. Right now, he's in very critical condition, and he may not survive this."

Words that, as a parent, you can't fathom hearing.

Remember my appointment with the psychic medium and the rainbow he was insistent that I pay attention to? As we sat waiting to be allowed back into Alex's ICU room around 5:00 a.m.—exhausted, heartbroken, and in shock—my husband suddenly spoke in an almost eerie tone.

"Look up at the window," he said.

Startled by his tone, I hesitated and looked at him, unsure. He repeated, "Look up at the window."

I followed his gaze, and there, in big letters across the top of the window, were the words: *#lookfortherainbow.*

Instant chills flowed through me as I sat there speechless. For a brief moment, a strange sense of peace washed over me—completely out of place for the situation we were in, but undeniable. It was an indescribably impactful moment for my husband and me, as we sat stunned and in awe. In hindsight, I believe that was God's symbol of hope to us on our darkest day, and it was the defining moment when I realized there is something far beyond our human comprehension to all of our lives and stories. You will continue to see the rainbow weaving itself throughout my story, having a remarkable impact.

Throughout the day, things were rocky. At one point, we almost lost Alex, even with the machines keeping him alive. Then came the news we had feared most: Alex had no brain activity. The doctor told us, "He is basically already gone." Then he added, "I'll give you some time to decide what you want to do next."

With heavy hearts, we made the heartbreaking decision to prepare to unplug the machines. We knew we needed to involve Alex's siblings. Alex's brother, who was fourteen, and his seven-year-old sister, whom he was very close to, needed to have the chance to say goodbye. His youngest sister, just two years old, was too young to understand, so we decided she would stay home.

Up to that point, Alex's siblings only knew that he was in the hospital. We wanted to tell them in person what was happening. My sister brought the kids to the hospital, and with the guidance of the hospital social worker, we prepared for the devastating conversation.

The social worker helped us navigate how to talk to them, offering support in the form of keepsakes: necklaces with Alex's name and a book called *The Invisible String*—another book that became a meaningful part of our family's journey through the heartbreak that was unfolding.

The kids arrived around 3:00 p.m. We sat them down and had to have another unimaginable conversation. We shared with them that Alex was going to go to heaven, so we wanted to give them the opportunity to say goodbye. It was a devastating moment as a mother—to share something that I knew would shatter their hearts while trying to hold myself together enough to give them space for their emotions.

Both of them chose to go into the room to say their goodbyes. My heart broke over and over with each painful step. Watching them say goodbye to their brother tore me apart in indescribable ways.

As I write this, I am overcome with emotion, being brought back to that day and the immense pain and sorrow that surrounded it.

After the kids left, we FaceTimed with some family members so they could say goodbye to Alex. Then my husband turned to me and said, "It's time." He went to get the doctor, and they began unhooking the machines.

As we prepared to say goodbye, I had a moment when I looked over at my husband standing on the left side of the bed, then down at Alex lying between us, and finally down at myself on the right side. I was overcome with emotion as I thought, *here we are on Mother's Day*—a day that symbolizes what Alex had longed for most in life: his mom—*and it is just Matt and me again by his side*, like it had been for the majority of Alex's life.

It broke my heart that Alex left this world on Mother's Day—a day that painfully mirrored his lifelong struggle with longing for his biological mom. That longing had always been a deep source of pain for him.

I want to take a moment to honor Alex's mom. Over the years, I have grown to hold her in my heart with love. Throughout Alex's life, I know she did the best she could to be there in the capacity she was able. Her heart was broken, too, and her pain deserves acknowledgment in this story of heartbreak. We are all doing the best we can with the circumstances and struggles we face, and Alex's mom is no exception.

Throughout his life, Alex and I shared a special bond. But I could never fill the void left by the longing for his mom—nor did I ever try to. I was his bonus mom. I cared for Alex to the best of my ability with the parenting skills I had at the time, though I fell short in many ways. My intentions were always good, and his well-being was at the heart of everything I did. I often say I did my "growing up" with Alex, since I was just eighteen when I began raising the boys alongside my husband.

Along the way, there were moments of deep closeness between Alex and me, as well as moments that brought tension. Over time, I've come to realize that Alex was my greatest teacher in my parenting journey. I'm deeply grateful for the lessons he taught me, which led to my growth and evolution as both a person and a parent.

In the final year of Alex's life, he carried anger and resentment toward me—some of it justified, some of it misplaced. This has been, and continues to be, a tremendous source of pain for me.

I loved Alex deeply, and the strain in our relationship during his final year weighed heavily on my heart. When he passed, the unresolved tension and lack of closure in our relationship tore me apart. The grief of losing him was compounded by the unfinished pieces of our story, leaving an ache I continue to battle with.

When my husband and I got married, we included a rose ceremony as part of our vows. Matt and I exchanged white roses, symbolizing our commitment to one another—an enduring promise to stay together no matter the obstacles we might face. The idea was that during tough times, we would give each other a white rose as a reminder of our vows and love for one another.

I gave the boys yellow roses, which symbolized my forever love and commitment to them. It was deeply important to me that the boys understood when I said "I do" to their dad, I was also vowing to be there for them always and to love them unconditionally as their bonus mom.

At 4:45 p.m. on May 9, 2021, as Alex's heart came to a stop, I stood by his side, something I had vowed and hoped to do until the end of my life, as surely he was supposed to outlive me. With immense love in my heart that spilled over as tears streamed down my face, I held his hand tightly.

That moment—standing by Alex's side, holding his hand as his heart stopped—is something I will hold very close to my heart for the rest of my life. It was a deeply heartbreaking experience, yet one filled with immense love. This tragic path has taught me that grief is love. As the saying goes, "Where there is deep grief, there was great love."

Although Alex's physical presence is gone, his spirit is deeply and intimately woven into the fabric of my life. His love, the lessons he taught me, and even the profound pain of losing him have become the center of my life's journey and the work I have been called to do. Through losing him, I've discovered a strength I never knew I had—a strength that allows me to carry the heavy weight of my grief while still embracing the enduring light of his love. His spiritual presence, often in the form of rainbows (which we will explore in the next chapter,) continues to guide me, reminding me that even in the deepest sorrow, love remains eternal.

PART 2

THE CAVE BEGINS TO TURN

Chapter 4

THE RAINBOW
BEYOND THE STORM

The mind is not equipped to process tragedy or profound difficulty on its own; it isn't built to withstand the enormity of such pain without support. In the face of overwhelming loss or hardship, our minds instinctively try to protect us through denial, suppression, or overanalysis. However, these mechanisms are only temporary, leaving the pain buried but unhealed. True healing requires going beyond the limits of thought and tapping into the deeper realms of faith, love, and hope—where the heart and soul provide what the mind cannot.

This chapter both explores how anchoring myself in these deeper realms transformed my grief and serves as proof that healing and transformation are possible for you too. Grief is a lifelong journey, but I have learned how to honor and carry it. Beyond your pain and hardships lies the opportunity to find purpose, hope, and renewal. By leaning into faith, love, and hope, I discovered purpose in my pain and began to navigate my way out of the cave of despair.

Life's storms often leave us shattered, searching for meaning amid the wreckage. After Alex's passing, I learned to survive by trusting and leaning into these deeper spaces. In doing so, I saw miracles begin to appear—most profoundly in the form of rainbows.

These rainbows have become more than fleeting natural phenomena; they are symbols of divine communication and Alex's presence. Each rainbow has met me in moments of darkness, gently illuminating the path toward healing and transformation. They remind me—and they can remind you—that even in the midst of overwhelming sorrow or struggle, there is always hope, light, and a higher purpose waiting to be revealed.

RAINBOWS: THE SYMBOL OF HOPE

The ICU moment when #lookfortherainbow appeared was the first spark of light in my cave. Little did I know this spark would grow into a steady flame, guiding me through grief, faith, and love. The rainbow became more than a beautiful arc in the sky—it became a divine language through which God spoke directly to my soul. Each rainbow served as a promise, assuring me that even through life's storms, beauty and healing await.

The night after Alex passed, this divine language became tangible. As my husband tucked our son Austin into bed, he pulled back the covers and there lay a small piece of paper with the word "rainbow" written in crayon. Stunned, he asked Austin where it had come from. Austin, confused and not understanding the significance said, "I don't know. I think Arie (our daughter) was writing her colors a while back." My husband, in awe, couldn't comprehend how that little piece of paper, written long ago, ended up there at that exact moment. The timing felt divinely orchestrated—a tender reminder that Alex and God were with us, offering hope in our shattered world.

From that moment on, rainbows began to appear during the most meaningful times, as if orchestrated by God to wrap us in love and comfort. Two weeks after Alex passed was his high school graduation—a day that should have been a celebration of his bright future. Instead, it was a day filled with unimaginable heartbreak. I sat in the stands, staring at the empty chair draped with Alex's cap and gown—the only vacant seat among a sea of excited graduates. Around us, parents beamed with pride, as we would have, yet there we sat in the shadows of darkness, feeling alone in a crowd of people celebrating, under the smothering blanket of grief and the pain that accompanied it. That night, the painful reality of Alex's absence cut deeply—a bright future gone in an instant. The weight of that evening, and the raw emotions it carried, will forever be etched in my heart. Yet, even in the midst of that darkness, my pain would continue to be met with the rainbow, illuminating the light and providing hope.

The next day, as I went to pick up Alex's cap and gown, the weight of the previous two weeks pressed heavily on me. I felt utterly defeated and broken. As I pulled into the parking lot and stepped out of the car, I walked alongside the vehicle next to me. Just as I rounded the corner, something caught my eye—a rainbow sticker in the back window. It stopped me in my tracks. For a moment, I felt held, as if God and Alex were wrapping me in a quiet, comforting hug. That small yet remarkable sign continued to serve as a reminder that even in the depths of sorrow there was a purpose, and their love and presence were near.

On Alex's eighteenth birthday—a day that loomed heavily over us—exactly two months after his passing, another rainbow appeared. As my husband and daughter drove into our neighborhood, a vivid arc stretched across the sky—another powerful moment of divine communication and love.

The first holidays brought another wave of grief. Thanksgiving was especially hard as I reminisced about Alex while going through family photos. In my reminiscing, I stumbled upon a picture I had never noticed before, one of our family in Vail, Colorado, the year prior. Around us in the photo was a rainbow-like ring. I couldn't believe it—it was the last picture we had of all six of us together.

Then Christmas Eve came. As we prepared to go to church, missing Alex immensely, a huge rainbow appeared outside our back window, stretching across our yard. It was as if God was reminding us continually that this journey will be stormy, and some days will be unbearably dark, but beyond the darkness there is light, and beyond the storm there are rainbows, a continued symbol of hope and beauty. These tender mercies—small yet profoundly meaningful signs of divine love—became beacons of hope during my darkest moments, steadily guiding me toward healing. They continue to weave themselves into our story almost four years later, showing up when we need them most, offering hope in the middle of our grief, and guiding us toward healing.

SURRENDER, FAITH, AND LOVE

Before sharing a few more powerful "rainbow moments," I want to pause and acknowledge the role of faith in my healing. Faith has been my anchor, a constant light through unimaginable darkness—a guide out of the cave. It has shown me that even in life's messiest moments, there is a divine presence working behind the scenes, weaving love and purpose into pain.

Again, this is not a book about religion, but it is a book about faith in something greater than ourselves. For me, that presence is God. For you, it may be Source, the Divine, the Universe, or Love itself. What matters is recognizing that this force is guiding us, offering hope and redemption even in our most broken places.

God showed up profoundly in my life right before Alex and Ty passed, using unexpected avenues to guide me. My fitness trainer led me to a church I initially resisted attending, but it ended up being everything I didn't know I needed. Then, I was introduced to a psychic medium whose insights shifted the trajectory of my grief, helping me uncover a deeper understanding of purpose through pain. These experiences transformed me from the inside out, giving me a voice to help others explore how their own pain and tragedies can be transformative and lead to a life of hope, healing, and purpose.

Faith led me to surrender—releasing the need to control outcomes and trusting in God's plan. Grace followed, teaching me to forgive myself and others. Love became the foundation of my healing—overcoming resentment, guilt, and shame. Tragedy and pain are constants in life, but they also hold the power to expand and deepen our souls, if we allow them to. To survive the inevitable challenges of this human experience, we must embrace faith, surrender, grace, and love. These virtues are lifelines connecting us to one another and lifting us out of despair.

RAINBOWS: THE CONTINUED MIRACLE

Rainbows continued to guide me well beyond the first year of Alex's passing, appearing in moments when I needed them most. Each one felt like a tender mercy, a reminder that God and Alex's presence are in every step of my journey.

In the previous chapter, I mentioned the rose ceremony from our wedding and its significant symbolism. Every year on our anniversary, I would give the boys a yellow rose as a reminder of my unconditional love for them. When we laid Alex to rest, I placed a yellow rose in his casket. We chose Vail, Colorado, as his final resting place—a place that holds profound meaning for our family. Vail has been a cherished destination since my childhood, a tradition we continued with our kids. Historically, we visited once annually, but now that Alex is there, we go several times a year.

In 2023, for the first time since Alex's passing, our trip coincided with our anniversary, allowing me to place a yellow rose on Alex's stone. It was a deeply meaningful moment that left my heart tender throughout the day. Later, I received a "random" text from a woman I met a year prior who had also lost her son to a fentanyl overdose. She shared a photo of a rainbow she'd seen that afternoon and wrote, "I wasn't sure who this was for, but 10 minutes later, you came to mind." It was exactly what my grieving heart needed that day—showing me that love transcends all barriers.

Another remarkable moment came in April of 2024 on my way to a women's retreat called "A Weekend of Surrender." Fittingly—or perhaps through divine intervention—the journey began with an opportunity to practice surrender. As I left town, a flat tire delayed me for hours. Frustration threatened to take hold, but I felt God urging me to trust there was a purpose in the delay, so I leaned in to that.

Finally back on the road, I drove into a torrential downpour, the rain so heavy I could barely see through the windshield. Again, frustration bubbled up, and I found myself asking, "God, why?" and thinking, *is this a sign I should turn around?* But as the rain began to lighten and the sun peeked through the clouds, I suddenly heard the words, "There's a rainbow."

Confused by the sudden thought, yet hopeful, I scanned the horizon. I looked ahead—nothing. I glanced out the left window—still nothing. Then, I turned to the right, and there it was: a vivid, breathtaking rainbow stretching across the sky.

Overwhelmed, I burst into tears.

That rainbow wasn't just a fleeting moment of beauty. It was a continued reminder that there is a reason for everything, a divine reassurance that the delay and the challenges weren't without purpose. It wrapped me in Alex's love with a heart full of gratitude and faith, preparing me as I entered a weekend dedicated to surrender.

The journey to write this book was yet another divine experience. One evening, after having dinner with a friend and telling her the story about the psychic medium and the rainbows, she said, "You should write a book." Though I had always thought I might write one someday, it wasn't something I planned to do anytime soon. Yet, that night I felt a strong nudge, different than I had felt before when the topic of writing a book came up. Within a week, without seeking or trying, God placed my publisher and business coach, Keira Brinton, on my path, and I found myself signed up for an author's retreat in the

British Virgin Islands. Truly, I sat in awe as it all unfolded so quickly and seamlessly. All I did was follow God's lead, and He made the rest happen, even working out the funds for the trip.

When I set out on this adventure, a deep wound surrounding Alex's passing resurfaced unexpectedly during the flight. By the morning after my arrival, my heart felt raw and tender. I sat on the breathtaking patio surrounded by the majestic ocean, as grief weighed heavily on me. I began to pray and journal about the wound. In between writing and praying, I would look out to the ocean, giving space for God to work in my heart. During one moment of pause, I looked up and there, out over the ocean, stretched a spectacular double rainbow. Overcome with emotion, I quickly stood to my feet in awe. In that moment, I felt God's tender mercy and Alex's love wash over me. I felt God communicating that it was time to lay this wound to rest. Healing is a journey and this moment was another step toward healing. I realized that hanging on to this wound was only keeping me stuck in the illusion of "not being a good mother" or "not being enough." But the rainbow was another reminder to keep my heart moving toward love, light, and grace because that is what drives out the darkness and illusions that keep us stuck and brings us toward the battles that save and restore. This is where healing and transformation lie. That moment was everything I needed to take my healing to the next level.

A few days later, I attended an equine therapy session on the island. Horses have always brought me peace, so I looked forward to the session. The facilitator asked me what I hoped to gain, and I replied that I needed clarity surrounding my career and healing from the unresolved wounds surrounding Alex's passing—two very different but pressing concerns on my heart. As the session progressed, we focused on my career, but nothing about my grief had come up. Midway through, the facilitator excitedly said, "Oh, look! A rainbow!" I turned my head, and there it was—a stunning rainbow arching across the sky. In awe, I showed her the tattoo down my spine that reads, "Look for the rainbow," and explained its deep connection to my son. She paused and said, "Wow, I have chills. I rarely feel this in my work, but this is something special."

We stood there together, marveling at the rainbow. What made it extraordinary was that there had been no rain—it was a perfectly sunny day. Yet, the rainbow lingered for the entire session, only fading as we finished. I had never seen one last that long. In that moment, I felt God gently nudging me once again, reminding me that it was time to lay the wounds of Alex's passing to rest. It was yet another indescribably moving experience.

These moments, and countless others, have shown me that rainbows symbolize more than hope—they are promises. They remind me that even through life's most painful storms, there is hope waiting on the other side. Whether you call it God, the Universe, or something else, there is a divine presence in this world working to guide us, comfort us, and help us transform our pain into something meaningful. Rainbows continue to teach me that pain, like storms, are inevitable, but the sun will always shine again. No matter how dark the storm, the light is never gone completely. Our struggles are never the end of the story. There is always hope, always beauty, always the possibility of healing, and always a force beyond our human comprehension that we can find solace in.

Chapter 5

THE ALCHEMY OF SUFFERING: TURNING PAIN INTO PURPOSE

The moment Alex passed, our world shifted irreversibly. There is life before Alex left this physical world, and life after. Navigating the *after* has been a relentless rollercoaster—grief's sharp turns and steep drops threatening to consume me entirely. Yet, in the midst of it all, this journey has been one of profound revelations.

Losing a child undoubtedly breaks you. You're left trying to gather the shattered pieces, grappling with a pain that threatens to swallow you whole. Another grieving mother once described it that way, and I couldn't agree more. When we lose someone so deeply cherished, we mourn because where there is great love, there is also profound grief. Love and pain often walk hand in hand.

For me, this loss tore my heart wide open—wide open to uncover a greater purpose. Just before Alex passed, God showed up in ways I couldn't have anticipated. I wasn't searching for Him. I wasn't particularly interested in faith. And yet, He was there—preparing me for the painful path ahead, relentlessly pursuing me, showing me that even in the depths of tragedy, there is meaning.

Looking back on the entire journey—the timing of everything, the people placed in my path, the doors that opened—it all feels surreal. God knew I was about to enter one of the most painful chapters of my life, and over these past four years, He has spoken loud and clear: *There is purpose in the pain.*

That truth isn't easy to grasp in the depths of grief. Sometimes, it hardly makes sense. But God's unwavering presence has shown me—down to the core of my being—that no matter the tragedy, there is meaning in it all.

I think of it like childbirth. It was the most physically painful experience of my life, yet on the other side of that pain was the most precious gift—another piece of my heart. Now, I face the unimaginable, the most emotionally painful experience I have ever known. But even in this, I have been shown that beyond the storm, there are rainbows—signs of hope, promise, and new beginnings.

Life brings suffering we may never fully understand. No one gets through unscathed. I'll never comprehend why my son's path took such an abrupt turn, why he was called home so soon. But I humble myself before God, trusting that this is not how our story ends. There is more, far beyond what we can see or comprehend. And this is where I have learned to trust.

To trust the greater purpose.

Today, as a therapist working with individuals battling suicidality, I recognize how my pain has shaped me into a stronger soldier in the fight for life. Amid the losses I have already shared, I lost my brother in August 2020 to an overdose—just nine months before losing Alex. His death was ruled a combination of substances, but a high level of fentanyl was found in his system. As I've said before, this battle is heartbreakingly widespread, touching every life in some way. Alex's spirit, along with the other losses I have endured, fuels my work today, while God's guidance lights my path as I return to the battlefield each day.

It's remarkable to reflect on how that same psychic medium who identified the significance a rainbow was about to have in my life also predicted that I would specialize in treating individuals with suicidal thoughts. At the time, I didn't even know such a specialty existed. Yet, two years later, the school district I worked for "coincidentally" partnered with an outpatient suicide treatment center—the first of its kind. Once again, I found myself divinely led. Though I had no intention of leaving my role at the school, God had other plans. I was guided to become the clinical director of this center, where I now dedicate my days to helping save lives.

I've come to learn that there is an enemy of our souls at work in this world—one with a mission to steal, kill, and destroy. But just before Alex passed, God entered my life, and His presence transformed the path of my grief. *God saves.* He is the way, the truth, and the light. I have come to know this truth on a soul level.

One evening, while deep in the editing phase of this book, I felt a nudge to attend a program called Celebrate Recovery, at my church, to continue working through the pain of losing Alex. Exhausted, I almost didn't go. But that quiet whisper in my heart urged me forward.

That night, Hosanna Wong, a phenomenal speaker and author, shared her story. As she spoke, it felt as if God Himself was speaking directly into my soul. She described herself as a fighter—something that resonated deeply with me.

She spoke of how we often get caught up in the wrong battles—the ones the enemy distracts us with—and in doing so, we lose sight of the battles God has *called* us to fight. Her words struck a chord, bringing me back to a coaching session that occurred in the beginning days of writing this book.

In that session, my business coach, Keira Brinton, read my story back to me. Hearing my own words spoken aloud stirred something powerful inside me. Moved to tears, Keira asked, "Lindsay, how are you still standing?" Overcome with emotion, I realized I had been asking myself the same question.

Keira saw *me*—not just my story but the essence of who I am. She acknowledged the weight of my tragedies and the strength it takes to rise each day. Even in my pain and darkness, she said, "You continued to return to the battlefield to stand by those fighting to stay alive."

"I *see* you," she said.

And for the first time, I felt truly seen.

At that moment, I felt something click into place, as if my soul aligned with its purpose. I heard God say, *"You are a fighter. A soldier in my army, here to bring love, light, hope, and truth to a world that so desperately needs it."*

That moment crystallized something within me: fighting and helping others fight is all I've ever known. I realized it's the gift God gave me—a resilience and light that refuses to waver no matter how persistent the darkness is. It's a call to face the good fight, to confront the enemy's lies with God's love, light, and redemption.

Because I now know this:

The enemy's battles steal, kill, and destroy. But *God's battles?* They save, restore, and reveal the truth of who we are.

I am a soldier on that battleground, here to let God's love, light, and truth work through me, reaching into the places the enemy has tried to destroy.

But even the strongest soldiers get tired. There have been countless times I've wanted to quit. Then, I remember those I love who "lost" their battles with substance use and suicide. And in those moments, God whispers to my heart:

"The battle was never lost."

Their fight lives on in me. It fuels me to stay in the fight—to show up, day after day, for those struggling to see the light. Because I now know that *God's love saves.* It brings us back to the truth of who we are: deeply loved, worthy, and whole.

When life deals you a blow so hard it drops you to your knees, you're in the perfect position to pray. Sometimes, prayer is all you have. And perhaps, it's all you need. Because in those moments—when the heart shatters—the soul learns to fly.

Writing this book has taken me back to the darkest corners of my battlefield. Losing a child could have broken me completely. And at times, it nearly did. But it was in the breaking that I became a stronger soldier. The pain, loss, and tragedies I've endured have pushed my soul to expand in ways I never imagined. Without descending into the depths of that dark, lonely cave, I wouldn't truly understand what it takes to survive life's darkest moments.

As our story continues to unfold, my heart will never be whole again. But, through the grace of God I have come to find acceptance in this journey—one that Alex now walks alongside us as our angel. I trust that God knew our hearts needed him in a different way. There is no mistake in God's plan for my story or yours.

The fact that you are reading this is no accident. As I reflect on every chapter that led me to this moment, I see now that everything had to happen exactly as it did—the highest highs, to the lowest lows—to reveal God's hope, love, light, and redemption.

Perfectly imperfect.

Remarkably orchestrated.

Leading me closer to Him—the eternal home of my soul.

And in this, I have found the purpose in the pain.

Whatever battle you are fighting, I want you to know this: *Your pain is not the end of your story.* It is an invitation—to deepen your faith, surrender to the Divine, and trust in the purpose of your journey.

Storms will come. But so will rainbows.

And through it all, *you are never alone.*

Turn your energy to the good fight, soldiers. The world needs you in this army to reclaim the light and save lives. Your story—the one you are living right now—could very well be the turning point that saves someone else's life.

<h1 style="text-align:center">Chapter 6</h1>

GRIEVING WITH GRACE

Before we move into stories of hope—sharing the journeys of warriors who have overcome battles with addiction and suicidality—I want to take a moment to speak to those who have lost a loved one to suicide or addiction. Even if your loss is different, the reflections in this chapter on grief will likely resonate, as it is a journey we all face at some point.

At the end of this chapter, you'll find support networks with QR codes to guide you toward additional resources. I invite you to lean into what speaks to you as we explore the complexities of grief together.

Losing someone to suicide or addiction, specifically, is one of the most heartbreaking and challenging experiences a person can endure. The pain cuts deep, and it's often accompanied by overwhelming questions, guilt, and sorrow.

In the wake of such a loss, it's natural to get caught in cycles of "what if" or "if only," questioning whether you could have done more to "save" them. For some, these feelings are further complicated by the relationship itself. Addiction, like any other disease—such as cancer— wreaks havoc not only on the individual but also on their loved ones.

Losing someone to addiction or suicide adds layers of complexity, often bringing waves of conflicting emotions that can feel difficult to process.

You may feel immense love and sorrow for the person you lost, but you may also experience anger, resentment, or hurt because of how their choices or actions during their struggle impacted you. Addiction, in particular, takes so much, not just from the person battling it but also those who love and support them. This was true in my experience with Alex. While sadness was my predominant emotion after his death, I also felt hurt by some of the decisions he made and the things he said and did. These feelings didn't diminish my love for him but they added complexity to my grief.

In the therapy world, there's a concept called **dialectics**, which refers to the idea that two seemingly opposing emotions can coexist. You can feel deep love for the person you lost while also feeling anger or frustration. Both are valid, and both can be true at the same time.

It's important to remind yourself, however, that their struggles were not your fault. Their pain and the outcome of their battle were never a reflection of your love, care, or worthiness as their loved one. This is a truth I have had to revisit time and again as I've worked through my own grief after losing Alex.

Grieving someone lost to suicide or addiction is a uniquely complex and deeply personal journey. As you navigate this path, allow yourself the space to feel the full range of emotions without judgment. It's in this process that healing begins, not by erasing the pain but by learning to carry it with grace and love for both yourself and the person you lost.

HONOR YOUR GRIEF AND CARRY THEIR MEMORY WITH LOVE

Grief is as unique as a fingerprint—no two journeys look the same. This idea resonated deeply with me when I first heard it, and it's a powerful reminder to not compare your grief to anyone else's. How you grieve is entirely your own; there is no "right" way to do it.

Give yourself permission to grieve in the way that feels right for you. Allow yourself to experience the full range of emotions: sadness, anger, confusion, guilt, even moments of relief or numbness. All of these feelings are valid. Journaling, talking to a trusted friend, or seeking support from a counselor or grief group can provide a safe space to process these emotions. Grief is not a burden you have to carry alone; it truly takes a village. I have leaned on many different people and resources throughout my own grief journey, and that support has been invaluable.

Take time to honor your loved one in ways that feel meaningful to you. This can be a powerful way to stay connected to their light while navigating your own healing. For me, my loss has fueled my determination to fight against the darkness in this world. Honoring them can help transform your grief, allowing you to carry their memory forward in a way that brings healing, hope, and purpose. Their love will always be a part of you—and if you let it, it can flow through you, guiding the way you move through the world.

I recently heard a quote that resonated deeply:

"Activation WITHOUT integration equals dysregulation. Activation WITH integration equals expansion."

When we awaken something within ourselves—whether it's a new realization, deep emotions, or even healing energy—without properly processing and integrating it, we can become overwhelmed, scattered, or emotionally dysregulated. It's like unlocking a door but not knowing how to walk through it. However, when activation is met with intentional integration—through reflection, embodiment, and aligned action—it leads to transformation, or expansion.

Grief is one of the most profound activations we will ever experience. When we lose someone we love, emotions (pain, anger, guilt, sadness, and even moments of love and longing) surge like a storm. But if we don't allow ourselves to process and integrate these emotions, they can consume us, leaving us lost in suffering. However, when we choose to integrate our grief—honoring our emotions, seeking meaning, and channeling our pain into purpose—we undergo expansion. Instead of being destroyed by our loss, we rise through it. We find ways to honor our loved one's legacy by helping others, sharing our story, or turning our pain into a force for change. True healing isn't about forgetting or moving on; it's about transforming our grief into something that keeps their light alive in the world while also saving others from the darkness.

NOTE: I invite you to get out a journal or notebook to write your responses, or simply reflect on the following questions:

Ask yourself:

- How can I honor their life in a way that reflects the beauty of who they were?

- What legacy of love, kindness, or resilience can I carry forward in their name?

AN INVITATION TO RELEASE THE "WHAT IFS"

Death is "final," so it often leaves those left behind in a space of "what if's," grasping for what "should have been" or "could have been." It's natural to replay conversations or moments, wondering if you could have done something differently. But it's essential to understand that their struggles were a result of their pain that was unique to them and their life perspectives, *not* your actions or inactions. Their choices, or the outcome of their battle, rests in *their* hands, not ours.

Forgive yourself for not having all the answers or not being able to "save" them. The truth is, another person's struggle is bigger than us—we can't save anyone but ourselves. And even then, true salvation and freedom come through the Divine, lifting our souls beyond the illusions and darkness that keep us stuck. Extend grace to yourself as you navigate these emotions. Remember, you provided love throughout their life, and that love mattered—more than you may ever realize. This is something I have had to remind myself of again and again as I walk through the deep pain and guilt of Alex's passing. I hope that as you move through these pages, you feel the presence of love and the reminder that you are not alone.

SEEK CONNECTION AND SUPPORT

Connection is vital in all things. Healing happens in community. You don't have to navigate loss alone. Sharing your story and hearing from others who have walked a similar path can bring comfort, connection, and even inspiration. In the depths of grief and struggle, the presence of others who understand can be a lifeline.

That's why I created the **Soul Soldier Community**, an online sanctuary for warriors of the soul and those who stand beside them. Inspired by the mission of my podcast, *Soul Soldier Speaks*, this community is for those battling addiction, suicidal thoughts, and life's darkest challenges, as well as for the loved ones who support them and those who carry the grief of loss.

We honor the fighters, celebrate the survivors, and ensure the legacy of the fallen continues to inspire and uplift. Whether you are in the midst of your own battle, walking alongside someone in theirs, reclaiming your light and purpose, or carrying the weight of loss, you are not alone.

Together, we navigate the battlefields of the mind and soul, offering hope, strategies, and unwavering support. I encourage you to join the online Facebook community and follow the podcast, as we reclaim the light, one soul at a time. Below are the QR codes to join.

Facebook Community:

Soul Soldier Speaks Podcast
(also available on Spotify and Apple Podcasts):

Website
(for resources and additional support):

EMBRACING HEALING: CARRYING LOVE FORWARD

Healing is a journey, not a destination. Some days will feel heavier than others, and that's okay. Give yourself grace as you navigate your grief. Focus on small, intentional steps: nourishing your body through things like movement, nature, and nutritious food while caring for your nervous system with things such as breathwork, meditation, and moments of stillness.

Your loved one would want you to live a life filled with love, light, and purpose. By choosing to heal, you honor their memory and carry their love forward in a way that transforms both you and the world around you.

Their absence will always be woven into your story, but it does not have to overshadow the love, growth, and purpose still within you. Over time, you can learn to integrate their memory in a way that fosters growth and renewal. Moving forward does not mean leaving them behind—it means carrying them with you, honoring the sharp edges of grief while making space for love, grace, and healing.

Together, we can hold space for the complexities of both loss and healing. Through this journey, we can transform pain into purpose, honoring both the love we shared and the resilience we carry within us.

Chapter 7

HOPE BEYOND THE CAVE

Healing requires confronting our pain and allowing the emotions we feel to move through us. This means allowing ourselves to feel the full weight of our emotions. I once heard it said that the word emotion stands for "energy in motion." Emotions are chemical processes in the body, typically lasting around 90 seconds IF we allow the emotion to be felt and thus move through our body.

The struggle arises when we suppress our emotions or create unhelpful interpretations of our emotions, instead of observing them and processing them in a healthy, non-judgmental manner. As a result, they end up staying stuck inside of us, which can have a lasting, negative impact on our mental and physical health. When a person allows an emotion to last for hours or days, it can become a mood. When the emotion lasts for weeks or months, it can become a temperament. And when it lasts for years, it can become a personality trait. Our brain develops neural pathways through learning, experiences, and time, so when people get stuck in negative emotions, the brain strengthens those pathways. We often underestimate the harm that is done when we suppress our emotions and do not process them and allow them to move through us.

RIDING THE WAVE: PROCESSING EMOTIONS WITHOUT GETTING STUCK

The key to processing emotions in a healthy way is practicing **mindfulness**—cultivating a non-judgmental awareness of your emotions as they arise. Often, we automatically label emotions as **"good"** or **"bad,"** which can send us into a spiral of unhelpful thinking. When we resist or suppress emotions because we believe we "shouldn't" feel them, they don't disappear; instead, they intensify, often manifesting as ongoing distress, anxiety, or even physical symptoms.

Instead of resisting emotions, we must learn to **ride the wave**—a concept from Dialectical Behavioral Therapy (DBT) that teaches us to allow emotions to flow naturally, without letting them consume or define us. Emotions, like waves, rise, peak, and eventually fall away. When we stop fighting against them or attaching unnecessary meaning to them, they pass through us more easily, reducing their intensity over time.

How to Ride the Wave of Emotion

1. Notice the emotion without judgment.

When a strong emotion arises, pause and acknowledge it without labeling it as "good" or "bad." Instead of reacting, simply observe:

- "I am feeling sadness."

- "I am experiencing frustration."

Naming the emotion gives you a sense of control and awareness rather than letting it overwhelm you.

Guided Exercise: Naming the Emotion

- Close your eyes and take a deep breath.

- Notice what emotion is present in your body.

- Without judgment, name the emotion. You might say, "I am noticing sadness in my chest," or "I feel anger rising in my stomach."

- Take a few more deep breaths, simply observing the emotion without trying to change it.

2. Allow yourself to feel without attachment.

Rather than pushing the emotion away or overanalyzing it, allow yourself to feel it fully. Imagine it as a wave—let it rise and crest, knowing it will also recede. Remind yourself that emotions are temporary; they are **meant to be felt, not feared.**

Example: A Wave of Grief

You feel a wave of grief coming on after hearing a song that reminds you of your loved one. Instead of suppressing it, you sit with the feeling. You close your eyes, take slow breaths, and say to yourself, "This is grief, and it's okay to feel it." You let yourself cry, allowing the emotion to move through you. After a few minutes, the intensity of the feeling begins to lessen, like a wave rolling back into the ocean.

3. Separate the emotion from the story.

When we feel strong emotions, our minds often create stories around them:

- "I feel anxious, which must mean something bad is going to happen."

- "I feel angry, so I must be a bad person because I feel this way."

These thoughts can keep us stuck. Instead, practice noticing the emotion as a **sensation** in the body rather than attaching a meaning or story to it.

Guided Exercise: Observing without Storytelling

- Sit quietly, and notice an emotion you're feeling.

- Instead of thinking about **why** you feel this way, focus on **where** it shows up in your body.

- Describe the sensation: "There is tightness in my chest," or "I feel heat rising in my face."

- Remind yourself, "This is just an emotion. It is not who I am."

4. Use your breath as an anchor.

When emotions feel overwhelming, bring your attention to your breath. Take slow, deep breaths and focus on the inhale and exhale. This helps regulate your nervous system and reminds your body that it is safe to experience emotion without reacting impulsively.

Example: Managing Overwhelm with Breathwork

You feel a rush of anxiety before attending a grief support group. Your heart races, and your thoughts spiral. Instead of letting the anxiety take over, you practice **box breathing**:

- Slowly inhale for 4 seconds.

- Hold for 4 seconds.

- Slowly exhale for 4 seconds.

- Hold for 4 seconds.

After a few rounds, your body begins to relax, and the emotion feels less overpowering.

5. Engage in movement or release.

Emotions are energy in motion. Sometimes, allowing them to flow requires a physical release—whether that's taking a walk, stretching, shaking out your hands, or journaling your thoughts. Expressing emotions in a healthy way prevents emotions from getting stuck in your body.

Example: Using Journaling to Release Emotions

If you're struggling with anger or frustration, set a timer for five to ten minutes, and write without censoring yourself. Let the words flow freely, releasing what's inside. When you're done, you can choose to keep the journal entry, tear it up, or toss it away as a symbolic release.

6. Trust that the wave will pass.

Every emotion has a natural lifespan. Just as no wave in the ocean lasts forever, no feeling stays at its peak indefinitely. Trust that if you allow it to flow, it will soften and fade, making space for new emotions and experiences.

Guided Exercise: Visualizing the Wave

- Close your eyes, and picture your emotion as a wave in the ocean.

- Imagine it rising, peaking, and then slowly rolling back into the sea.

- As the wave recedes, take a deep breath and remind yourself, "This emotion is passing, just like a wave."

FINAL THOUGHTS: EMBRACING EMOTIONAL FLOW

By practicing **riding the wave**, you develop emotional resilience—the ability to **feel fully, process effectively, and move forward without getting stuck in cycles of distress.** Instead of fearing emotions, you learn to trust their natural rhythm.

Over time, this practice helps you build confidence in your ability to navigate even the most intense emotions with grace and self-compassion. You are not your emotions; you are the observer, riding the waves, allowing them to come and go while staying grounded in your own strength.

Facing our struggles requires courage, but it is the only way to release their grip. By walking through the darkness rather than running from it, we take back our power and give ourselves the opportunity to process, learn, and grow.

Avoidance might seem like a safe route, a way to escape the sharpness of pain, but it's a false refuge, a shadow that follows us while whispering reminders of what we've pushed aside. Numbing the pain—with distraction, substances, or emotional detachment—only freezes it in place. It waits for us, unchanged, until we're ready to face it. Escapism is at the core of addiction and suicidality, and its power keeps us suffering. Healing doesn't come from sidestepping tragedy but from facing it and moving through it. I understand firsthand that the journey is not easy, but it is transformative. It allows us to reclaim our power, reframe our experiences, and emerge stronger, more compassionate, and more connected to what truly matters.

Loss, trauma, and profound challenges stir deep emotions and leave lasting marks, but they also open pathways for transformation. These experiences expand our hearts and, if we allow them, shift our perspectives—revealing that hope can exist even in the midst of great pain. While much in life is beyond our control, we hold the power to choose our response. It is in the depths of suffering— with an open heart— that we can uncover the catalysts for true growth and self-expansion.

The losses I have faced have fundamentally reshaped my life, altering my priorities and deepening my understanding of life's fragility and what truly matters. Through this journey, I continue to learn how to channel my emotions in a way that keeps me moving forward—without attaching unnecessary meaning or suffering to the emotions themselves.

Chapter 8

UNSEEN WARRIORS

Beyond my own journey, I am deeply inspired by the resilience of others I've encountered—those who have faced their darkest days and emerged stronger. If I asked you who your hero is, what would you say? Heroes come in many forms—superheroes, veterans, parents, siblings, friends, or mentors. *My* heroes are the unseen warriors who battle on the frontlines of their own lives, often overlooked in their courage. These individuals have fought addiction, battled suicidality, stepped through the heavy weight of grief and life's hardships, and still chosen life. These are among the hardest battles a person can face, and finding hope and purpose on the other side is nothing short of heroic.

If you are in the midst of your own fight—and still here despite the darkness—you are my hero. Staying in the fight takes immense courage, especially when the weight of pain feels insurmountable. In this chapter, I'll share the stories of remarkable people I've had the honor of getting to know, individuals who have faced their battles and eventually chosen to walk through their struggles rather than run from them.

These warriors didn't find an easy road, and their stories don't imply the fight is over. Sobriety, healing, and choosing life often requires continued effort, but these warriors reached a place where the darkness no longer controls them. They took their power back. Through resilience, courage, and faith, they've uncovered lives filled with hope and light. Their journeys are a testament to the possibility of transformation, reminding us all that no matter how overwhelming the struggle, there is always a path forward.

Let their stories inspire you to keep going, to hold on to the belief that even in the deepest pain, a brighter future is possible. You, too, are capable of reclaiming your power and finding the light.

ISREAL'S STORY: A HARD-FOUGHT, HARD-WON BATTLE

Let me start with my friend Isreal. You may recall the adoption agency I mentioned earlier. Israel was the husband of one of the birth moms I worked with, though they have since divorced. He was in prison serving a seven-year sentence when I first met this birth mom, Ava (whose name I've changed to protect her privacy). I stayed in touch with Ava after my time at the agency ended. I eventually met Isreal after his release from prison.

One night, Ava called me in distress. She explained that Isreal was struggling and in a dark place—convinced people were after him—and he was at risk of harming himself. Desperately, she asked if I could come. This would mark the beginning of a story about the relentless fight for life, the courage to face darkness, and the transformative power of grace—a testament to the truth that all things and people can be redeemed.

Feeling a strong pull to help, I agreed to go, asking my husband, Matt, to come with me since I wasn't sure what I'd be walking into. When we arrived, Isreal was just as Ava had described: paranoid and in a drug-induced psychosis. Matt and I managed to get Isreal into the backseat of our car and began talking with him, trying to assess the situation and determine the best course of action.

It quickly became clear that Isreal was both paranoid and suicidal; he was in urgent need of help. He slipped in and out of lucidity, but eventually, he agreed to go to the hospital with us. During the drive, he repeatedly asked if we had a gun and begged to borrow it; he was terrified that people were coming after him, and he wanted to end it before they reached him. We reassured him that we were taking him to a safe place for the night.

That night, at the hospital, Isreal hugged Ava, thanked Matt and me for helping him, and, despite his mental instability, took the brave step to seek help. It was a moment of courage amid the chaos—a glimmer of hope in the darkness.

A few days later, Isreal called to express his deep gratitude for what we had done for him. He said, "You guys don't even really know me, and yet you came and saved me. I'm just super grateful for your kindness in saving a stranger's life."

While Isreal wasn't a complete stranger to us, I hadn't spent much time with him. I know it was God who placed us there that night to help him keep fighting for his life. I remain humbled by every situation

God has positioned me in to help someone stay in the fight for their life.

It can be difficult to walk alongside people in their darkest moments, to come face-to-face with the battle of the enemy, but words cannot capture the profound beauty of meeting people in the middle of their cave and witnessing God work—sometimes directly and sometimes through others—to restore people and bring them back to life. It's incredible to see God's grace and light shine upon their lives, restoring hope and purpose in ways only He can.

That night was just the beginning. Isreal continued to face darkness and battle for his life, but on February 12, 2021, he took a courageous step and sought help one final time. That day marked the beginning of his journey to sobriety—a journey that has led him to a life beyond his wildest dreams.

In honor of his four years of sobriety, I want to share a post Isreal wrote on Facebook. In it, he recounts his journey, his decision to stay and seek help at the treatment facility he attended, and the pivotal role his friend and the program played in helping save his life. It's a testament to how God continued to place the right people and opportunities on his path, while Isreal did his part to stay in the fight for his life.

Isreal said,

Ian and Crossroads Arcadia saved my life. (1st attempt) Ian ate the poison pizza and stopped the family with the baby parked behind us from robbing me . . . he took my broken buttery knife!! (2nd attempt) I called Ian [while I was] hanging off the side of a freeway because the invisible cops and bad people were after me. He said, "You're going to jail." (3rd attempt) At Crossroads, after the mental institution let me out because I'm not crazy, he said those words that I'll never forget!!! (JUST STAY)—Love you, Ian! I'm not the perfect sponsee, but because I stayed, I found myself and a life I couldn't have dreamed of.

Since then, Isreal has fallen in love, remarried, and reunited with his children. He has a great job and is living a life he's proud of. Matt and I were honored to attend his wedding in February 2023—a beautiful evening filled with love and hope. As I stood there that night, I couldn't help but reflect on the journey Isreal had taken. From being with him on one of his darkest days to witnessing one of his best, I stood in awe of his transformation.

When I asked Isreal if I could share his story in this book and if he had anything he wanted to say, this was his heartfelt response:

It is God, Lindsay. I chose to finally give Him all of me. God overpowered the voices and grip of sin. I only had to rid all the trash within, and it was painful because it was me in the way of God's plan the whole time. I hated me the most because of the things I couldn't control as a child or in life as I grew. I was the mastermind behind my own suffering. God is behind what you are doing. Family, I am so honored to be of service.

Isreal's story is a powerful testament to a hard-fought, hard-won battle—a story of hope and the possibility of a better life. It's yet another example of God's love and grace, transforming even the darkest pasts.

No matter what your journey has been—whether it includes prison, addiction, relapses, or years of struggling to choose life—there is hope for you. There is hope for a life you can be proud of, one that can exceed your wildest dreams.

I have story after story that affirms this truth. These stories are a part of my "why"—the reason I continue to return to the battlefield to help people fight for their lives. I have come to deeply know the power of bringing God's love and light to these battlefields, and through this I've witnessed how the cave turns, revealing a life of endless possibility on the other side. Hope is real, and transformation is possible.

RANDY'S BATTLE AND BREAKTHROUGH: FINDING LIFE AGAIN

The next warrior I want to introduce is my dear friend Randy. When I met Randy and his girlfriend, Mandy, they had both recently been released from jail, were battling substance use, and working to rebuild their lives.

On January 11, 2018, they welcomed their daughter, Delilah, into the world—a blessing that brought hope and new beginnings into their lives.

For several years after Delilah was born, Mandy and Randy did well. They had a home, and Randy ran his own upholstery business out of their garage. During this time, we kept in touch and my family and I attended Delilah's birthday parties each year, celebrating the bright milestones of their journey.

In August 2022, I received a call from Mandy. Their landlord had given them a 30-day notice, and they were struggling to find housing due to a prior felony conviction and lack of savings. On the day they lost their home, Mandy asked if we could take Delilah for the weekend while they figured out their next steps.

That weekend stretched into a couple of months, during which we intermittently cared for Delilah as Mandy and Randy moved between weekly rentals, trying to find stability. Eventually, the situation became rocky, and I had to set boundaries. This led to us losing contact for about nine months.

Then, on August 3, 2023, I received an unexpected call from Mandy and Randy. The Department of Children's Services (DCS) had intervened and was removing Delilah from their care. They asked if Matt and I could take her, and without hesitation, we agreed.

For the next fourteen months, we fostered Delilah while walking alongside Mandy and Randy as they worked to rebuild their lives. The journey was anything but easy. For the first four months, Randy struggled deeply with his mental health, haunted by his past and years of guilt, shame, and trauma that resulted in substance use and suicidal thoughts.

By December 2023, he hit rock bottom. One night, Mandy called me in fear—Randy was walking into oncoming traffic and saying he wanted to end his life. It was then that I learned he had been using fentanyl for years. Randy was volatile, suicidal, and in desperate need of detox and treatment.

The situation was fragile, but we managed to intervene. An involuntary psychiatric hold was put in place, creating a window of hope. Soon after, Randy reached out to my husband, Matt.

"I'm ready to check myself into detox," he said.

Matt picked him up, and they talked. During that conversation, Randy poured out his heart. He admitted he was exhausted from the life he had been living and was ready to change—not just for himself but for his family and for Delilah. He gave Matt his word. "I'm done. I'm never going back."

Randy expressed immense gratitude for Matt's respect and support. Though terrified of the withdrawal process, Randy stayed in the fight and took the courageous step to walk through the door to detox. That moment marked the beginning of Randy's journey toward healing and redemption.

REDEMPTION THROUGH GRACE

Over the next nine months, Matt and I witnessed Randy's remarkable transformation. He and Mandy began attending church with us, and faith became a cornerstone of Randy's healing journey. God's grace helped him confront and work through years of guilt and shame, shining light into the darkest corners of his past and leading him to a place of redemption.

I watched as Randy transformed from an angry soul weighed down by darkness into a gentle, genuine man filled with goodness and love. His change was profound—a true testament to God's love, as well as his own dedication, faith, and hard work.

On September 20, 2024, Randy's journey came full circle. After years of battling substance use and the heartbreak of losing two other children to DCS, he and Mandy experienced the greatest blessing as a result of their perseverance and faith: they were reunited with Delilah.

That night, Matt and I had the humbling honor of placing Delilah back into their arms. It was a remarkable moment, a moment of pure grace, a true miracle, and a powerful reminder of the beauty that can emerge from even the darkest battles.

To mark the deeply profound and emotional occasion, I wrote this social media post:

Hey there, Delilah . . . It's only fitting I start this post with your favorite song, the song you were named after. Sweet girl, I hope you never lose sight of how special you are. You will forever hold a very special place in our hearts. Thank you for bringing so much love and joy to our home these last 14 months. Loving and caring for you has been a blessing and something we will always cherish.

Over a year ago, Delilah joined our family while her parents worked very hard to improve their lives and situation to bring her back home. Friday night, Delilah went back home. I am so very PROUD of her parents, Mandy and Randy, my dear friends. Delilah's bond with her parents is a true testament to their love and care for her despite the circumstances that led her to us.

Sadly, most parents who lose their kids to DCS do not get them back. It is not lost on me how hard Mandy and Randy worked to bring their girl back home AND the POWER of God's redemption. This experience has humbled me to deeply know what it is to be human and to be humane. To witness people's capacity for courage, resilience, endurance, and change is a profound gift. When we change our lives, we change our families. When we change our families, we change our communities. And when we change our communities, we change the world. I end this chapter with a grateful heart. Grateful for it ALL. Mandy and Randy's transformation has been nothing short of amazing. All thanks be to God.

THE HUMANIZING LENS: BELIEVING IN TRANSFORMATION

As I reflect on this journey, I am brought back to the day Delilah came to live with us—a day that powerfully reminded me of the importance of never counting anyone out. It's a call to extend grace, offer forgiveness, and resist writing people off based on their past or present circumstances. It challenges us to set aside assumptions and judgments that dehumanize and instead embody and embrace a perspective that humanizes and dignifies others.

What I'm about to share does not diminish the seriousness of abuse or neglect, nor does it minimize the consequences of such actions. Instead, it's about shifting our mindset—moving from seeing people and their situations as hopeless to recognizing them as imperfect humans, like all of us, who are capable of profound transformation and healing.

When the caseworker brought Delilah to us, she looked at my husband and said, "This is a bad one. You and your wife better start having some serious discussions about adopting her." From the outset, she had written Mandy and Randy off, assuming Delilah would never return home. Their circumstances were undeniably challenging, their history marked by repeated struggle and failure. But Mandy and Randy's story is a powerful reminder of an essential truth: no matter how many times you fall or how difficult the past may be, transformation and life change are always possible.

I want to extend grace to that caseworker. Her job is unimaginably hard, filled with tragic realities that most of us cannot begin to comprehend. I began my own career in Child Protective Services, so I know firsthand how overwhelming and emotionally draining this work can be. Burnout in this field is a very real and understandable challenge. Still, it is my prayer that we, as a society, can begin to shift this mindset.

By embracing a humanizing perspective, we can move beyond seeing only the brokenness in people's lives to recognizing their inherent goodness and their potential for radical transformation, no matter how bleak their situation may seem. Such a shift could profoundly change lives in ways we cannot even imagine. When lives are transformed, so are our communities, creating a ripple effect of hope and renewal that touches far beyond the individual.

This perspective isn't limited to child welfare. Consider those in prison: they are often written off and deemed unworthy of redemption. But recognizing the inherent good in every person could be revolutionary. This doesn't excuse wrongdoing or negate the need for accountability—both are essential. But it does mean keeping the door open for those ready and willing to embrace a second chance. Grace, love, and proper support can lead to extraordinary outcomes for those who choose to receive them.

Mandy and Randy come over nearly every Sunday for family dinner. Randy continues to fight like the warrior he is, now a part of God's battle, battling for a better tomorrow. Together, we are a forever family, bonded by the miraculous work of God.

Randy's story is yet another testament of the radical life change that can happen, especially when we tap into those deeper spaces of faith, hope, and love. No matter what your past or present looks like, there is goodness awaiting you on the other side of the cave. Don't ever count yourself out. Stay in the fight, my warrior friends—you are just as capable as Isreal and Randy of building an incredible life and creating a tomorrow you believe in.

The next stories I want to share are about individuals who have fought to stay alive, even when addiction wasn't part of their journeys. These warriors have faced the struggle to simply live and discovered life waiting for them on the other side of their cave.

MEGAN'S STORY: FROM DARKNESS TO LIFE

Megan (name changed for confidentiality) was a student I worked with during my time at the high school. A sophomore who had just turned sixteen when we met, she came to know the **Wellness Room** —a classroom-turned-wellness space—where students could pause, reflect, or talk through their struggles. Inside that space was my office, a safe haven for those in need of support.

One Thursday in October of 2021, Megan entered the room, sat down in a chair, and began journaling. I gently approached her and asked if she needed to talk or just have some time to herself. She politely replied that she didn't need to talk. I assured her I was there if she changed her mind.

The next day, Megan returned and asked if I was available to talk. She sat down and began sharing pieces of her story and the struggles she faced. We ended up talking for over an hour. From that moment on, Megan became someone I supported regularly.

It wasn't until later that Megan revealed that when she first entered my classroom, she had been writing goodbye letters and planning to end her life that very weekend. She shared that meeting with me the next day changed everything. With heartfelt emotion, she said, "You saved my life that day."

Once again, I found myself divinely placed in someone's life, offering hope in a critical moment. But I expressed to Megan that it was her—she saved her own life by choosing to keep going. My role was simply to walk alongside her and support her as she continued the fight. These stories continue to prove to me that standing alongside someone, although you can't change their circumstance for them, can make all the difference. Never underestimate your role in helping others simply by being an unconditional supportive presence in their life.

Megan later recognized that she believed it was God's miraculous work that brought us together in that pivotal moment, connecting us when she needed it most.

Over the next few years, Megan battled intensely with suicidal ideation and even attempted suicide. Yet, she never stopped fighting. One day, she shared a story that marked a profound turning point in her journey, a moment that occurred before our paths ever crossed.

Megan recalled a day she had decided to end her life. She had been dirt-bike riding with her brother on a particularly difficult day, overwhelmed by the belief that no one cared about her. Driving home, she decided she was going to die by suicide when she got home, so she sent this message to a friend, "Nobody cares, I'm done," and then turned off her phone.

Immediately afterward, she looked up and saw a random billboard in the middle of nowhere that read, **"God cares."** It was a miraculous moment that stopped Megan in her tracks. Stunned, she felt the magnitude of God reaching out to her in her darkest moment. That encounter changed everything that day. She turned her phone back on, reached out to her friend, and asked about attending the next church service. Though her friend had invited her to church many times before, it was at that moment—when she felt God speaking directly to her—that she knew she needed to go.

Since that day, Megan has experienced more than one divine encounter like this. During her lowest points, she has felt God's presence showing up to guide her back to hope. It has been incredible to witness her resilience and her willingness to lean on faith and hope during her darkest moments.

For the next two years, I counseled Megan through some of the most challenging days of her life, striving to meet her on the battleground and help her uncover the light within herself. Her courage and bravery in sharing her story deserve the deepest honor, and I am privileged to include her words here.

I found myself in a place I never thought I would be—overwhelmed by despair and contemplating an end to my pain. In that quiet space, I sat with a heavy heart, writing letters of goodbye. I felt lost, convinced I was done. I didn't think there was any hope left.

But then Lindsay entered my life. She approached me gently and encouraged me to open up. I declined because I was planning to be done and continued to write my letters. The next day, something in me told me to find her and talk to her. That decision changed everything.

Lindsay helped guide me through some of my darkest memories, helping me unpack the pain I had been carrying. Truthfully, I think God sent her to help me through some of the hardest things. It was such perfect timing. Throughout our conversations, I began to discover strength within myself that I didn't know existed. With her support, I learned coping skills that changed my perspective on life.

We spent a lot of time talking about perspective—how staying focused on the negative for too long would only make things worse. I still have my hard days, but I've learned resilience, and suicide is no longer an option for me. Today, I'm proud to say I work as a Registered Behavior Technician (RBT) at a clinic where I've spent the past year helping others navigate their challenges. By doing this, I get to use my story to inspire others. I always told myself if I made it out of the dark spot I was in, I wanted to use my story as a guide to remind someone that even in the darkest places, there is always hope.

Today, Megan no longer struggles with suicidal ideation at the intensity she once did. While such thoughts occasionally arise, she has reached a place where suicide is no longer an option for her—a powerful testament to her incredible resilience and growth.

Megan's story is a powerful reminder that hope is always possible. Even when thoughts of suicide persist, they don't have to define or consume you. It is possible to hold space for those thoughts while still experiencing joy and gratitude for life—they can coexist.

This concept, known as dialectics (as previously discussed), teaches us that opposing truths can be equally valid. For me, it's one of the most transformative truths to embrace in life.

Megan is a warrior who has chosen life in the face of darkness. Her story serves as a beacon of hope for anyone who is struggling—proof that even in the depths of despair, there is a way forward into the light.

KEIRA'S STORY: THE POWERFUL IMPACT OF CHOOSING LIFE AND ACTING ON OUR PURPOSE

The next warrior I want to share with you is a powerhouse of a woman named Keira. This book likely wouldn't exist if it weren't for her decision to choose life. Keira has a profound passion for bringing transformative books into the world—books that change lives and make an enduring impact. She is unlike anyone I have ever met. Being in her presence feels sacred, as if you are standing in the glow of pure light.

Keira has an unparalleled ability to ignite passion and purpose in others, breathing life into every soul she touches. Her words move rooms, and her presence sparks transformation. But what makes her story so deeply moving is that she spent over twenty years battling suicidal thoughts—a struggle she still faces, though now they come less frequently.

Kiera takes authors on adventures to help them write their books. I was blessed to go on a life-changing, sacred island adventure with Keria to bring this book to life. During the island adventure, on a serene morning on the balcony of a breathtaking resort, Keira shared the deeply emotional and painful story of the day she almost ended her life. As always, Keira spoke words of inspiration and life into the group, her presence as luminous as the sunshine before us.

She opened up about her darkest moment—a day when she was lost in the depths of her own cave, consumed by despair and hopelessness. Her vulnerability silenced us all, and there wasn't a dry eye as we felt the weight of her story. We could sense the darkness that had once consumed her, dimming her light and hiding the immense goodness and potential within her that was waiting to be discovered.

As I listened to Keira's story, I was struck by the stark contrast. Here was this extraordinary person—leading a retreat, empowering women, building a business on the verge of eight figures, and embodying the hands and feet of God—revealing that she had once been so lost she wanted to end her life. It was a powerful reminder that even the brightest lights can find themselves in moments of significant darkness.

I sat there reflecting on the ripple effect of her choice to live. Had she not continued to fight, she wouldn't have reached the day that she is moving mountains and building a village of changemakers. Her decision to choose life, even in her darkest hour, didn't just save her; it has become a source of life for countless others. None of us would have been on that island, writing these transformative books, if Keira hadn't made the courageous choice to *stay*.

During the editing phase of this book, I attended an event Keira hosted for her authors and fellow women entrepreneurs. One day, while she was on stage passionately leading and sharing her wisdom, she had a profound realization. She said, **"I have the gift of ideation."** The words stopped her in her tracks. After a brief pause, she added thoughtfully, "Interesting."

In that moment, Keira recognized that she often receives powerful visions of things she is meant to create. However, when she doesn't follow through on those visions, the creative energy becomes trapped, transforming into suicidal ideation. This stuck energy creates a deep sense of misalignment stemming from not fulfilling her purpose. This directly relates to the quote I shared earlier, "Activation WITHOUT integration equals dysregulation. Activation WITH integration equals expansion."

Keira's realization was transformational, shedding light on why some people remain trapped in cycles of suicidal thoughts. Even when activation without integration doesn't lead to suicidality, it often results in burnout or deep suffering. When we ignore or suppress our emotions, visions, or callings, we fall out of alignment with our soul's true desires and purpose. The energy meant to move through us becomes blocked, creating a void that leaves us feeling empty, inadequate, and lost. As the quote suggests, receiving inspiration without acting on it leads to inner turmoil. But when we integrate and embody what our soul is calling us to create, we step into alignment, experiencing expansion instead of suffering.

Keira's story is a testament to the power of resilience and living a life in alignment with our purpose. Her journey reminds us that no matter how dark or hopeless our lives get, we are here on purpose *with a purpose,* and tapping into that purpose can save our life. To the person reading this, you are worthy beyond measure. Within you lies a power and purpose waiting to be claimed. You belong, and you are needed.

Lean in, dig deep, and do the work to uncover the beautiful future that awaits you. Like Keira, you have the potential to create a ripple of impact that changes lives—starting with your own.

BRITNIE'S STORY: A MISSION OF HEALING

The next inspiring woman I want to share with you is Britnie, the owner of the island where I wrote this book. Britnie is a force to be reckoned with, renowned for her humanitarian work through the nonprofit she founded, **Aerial Recovery**. This remarkable organization spearheads numerous impactful efforts, including **Heal the Heroes**, which helps veterans and first responders find healing after returning to civilian life. They also engage in disaster response, animal rescue, and anti-human-trafficking missions, making an astounding difference in countless lives.

Our first night on the island, Britnie shared with us a brief yet extraordinarily moving piece of her journey. She captivated the room with her presence and sincerity as she recounted how she came to own the island—a story filled with determination, struggle, faith, miracles from God, and an unwavering vision to transform the island into a sanctuary for healing. Her words carried a powerful resonance, drawing everyone into the heart of her mission.

As she spoke, Britnie revealed a deeply personal moment, and it touched everyone in the room. She described a night a few years prior when she was standing on the balcony of her apartment, overwhelmed by despair, contemplating ending her life. The raw vulnerability of her confession was a stark contrast to the confident, compassionate leader we saw before us. She acknowledged that miracles from God along the way played a vital role in her journey to overcoming her dark times and getting to where she is today.

I was struck by the profound paradox: here was another beautiful, powerful woman dedicating her life to saving others, yet she had faced a moment of such darkness that she questioned whether her own life was worth saving. That moment served as a sobering reminder that no one is immune to the struggles of life—struggles that can lead even the strongest among us to the brink of suicidality or addiction.

Britnie's story is a testament to the hidden battles so many fight behind closed doors. It underscores the importance of creating spaces for healing, connection, and hope—spaces like the sanctuary she envisions for her island. Her courage to share such a vulnerable chapter of her life not only inspires but also challenges us to look at the world with greater compassion and awareness. It reminds us that even those who appear to have everything may be carrying unseen burdens, and it calls us to offer kindness, understanding, and support to everyone we meet.

The next morning, I reflected on Britnie's story. If she had not chosen to keep living, the countless lives she has since helped and saved through her humanitarian work would not have been impacted. She wouldn't have experienced the joy of bringing her beautiful son into the world. Her decision to stay not only transformed her own life but also created a ripple effect that continues to touch the lives of many.

In a quiet moment of reflection, I felt God put it on my heart to speak directly to those who are successful, influential, and outwardly appear to "have it all." These individuals often occupy positions of admiration and respect, yet they, too, can find themselves in places of suffering. Their struggles can be hidden behind outward achievements, their pain veiled by accolades and outward success.

Britnie's story is a poignant reminder that suicidality knows no boundaries—it does not discriminate based on wealth, status, or accomplishments. It can affect anyone, no matter how many lives they've touched, how much good they've done, or how far-reaching their influence may be. The truth is, the darkness can creep in quietly, even into lives that seem filled with light from the outside.

This underscores an important reality: no one is immune to the weight of despair. It's a call for us to see beyond appearances, to recognize the humanity behind success, and to extend grace and support to *everyone*. Britnie's journey speaks powerfully to the need for understanding, compassion, and the courage to face the darkness, regardless of where we are in life or what we possess.

Britnie also shared about her husband, a veteran in recovery who battled greatly with addiction and suicidal thoughts. His journey is one of complete transformation. Together, he and Britnie now work side by side, dedicating their lives to humanitarian efforts and saving others. His story is yet another example of someone who climbed out of despair to build a life of purpose and impact.

I continue to be deeply moved by the incredible transformations these warriors have experienced, not only in their personal lives but also in the far-reaching impact of their work. The lives they have touched and saved are immeasurable, and their stories serve as powerful reminders of the hope and healing that become possible when one commits to the hard work of healing and choosing life even in the darkest places. I will conclude this chapter with one more inspiring story about a remarkable woman I met on the island: Veronique.

VERONIQUE'S STORY: CHOOSING TO STAY, CHOOSING TO RISE

On the night we arrived, we gathered around a beautiful table at the top of the island, sharing a gourmet meal while taking in the breathtaking views. It was an evening of introductions, with each of us taking turns sharing about our books and the purpose that had brought us to this sacred place.

Veronique sat next to me, and when her turn came, she hesitated. With quiet vulnerability, she shared that she wasn't entirely sure why she was there. But she had felt a deep, undeniable calling to this island and knew in her soul she needed to answer it, so she did.

As Veronique shared her doubts, I couldn't help but notice the radiance of her soul—a special gift waiting to be fully discovered. Her authenticity and grounded presence stood out, refreshing and deeply moving.

The next day, we sat together at lunch, looking out over the serene ocean. Our lighthearted conversation began with laughter as we bonded over being "leadfoots" when we drive. The night before, I had introduced myself as "Loving Lindsay" but joked that my friends often call me "Leadfoot Lindsay." What started as playful banter soon shifted to a deeper connection when Veronique confided in me.

Just a month before coming to the island, Veronique had been suicidal. She recounted a harrowing day when she ran down the hallway to her room, screaming in desperation at her friend to remove her guns from the house. "Never leave me a loaded gun," she begged, "because I will blow my head off." Tragically, her nine-year-old son overheard her cries. Through tears, she threw the guns to the floor, demanding that her friend take them away. Her vulnerability with me was both heartbreaking and inspiring.

As I listened, I just saw greatness in this woman. It reminded me of my reflections on Britnie's story earlier that morning during my prayer time. Once again, I was struck by the reality that no one is immune to the darkness. Here we were, in the middle of paradise, surrounded by unimaginable beauty and peace, yet the weight of suicidality had found its way into this sacred space.

Vernique ended up having a life-changing moment the next day when she began to step into her power and purpose. It was beautiful to witness the beginning of her unfolding and transforming her pain into purpose.

This experience on the island continued to make one truth abundantly clear: it doesn't matter who you are, what you have, or where you come from—no one is immune to the battles of the soul. The struggles of life are part of our shared humanity, and we all fight battles, sometimes unexpected and often unseen.

Veronique's courage to show up—to step into the light of this island retreat despite her recent darkness—is a testament to the resilience that lives within each of us. When we discussed including her story in this book, Veronique shared a deeply personal memory about a close friend, who was like a sister to her, whom she lost to suicide—a friend who had faced significant medical challenges. In reflecting on the stigma surrounding suicide, Veronique noted how society often labels those who struggle with or lose their battle to suicide as "selfish."

It is my hope that, through this book, we can collectively challenge that misconception. The truth is, staying in the fight for life is one of the most courageous battles a person can face. For those we tragically lose to this battle, their passing does not diminish the strength and resilience they displayed while navigating the immense challenges of life.

We must begin to view these losses through the same compassionate lens we reserve for those who fight and lose their battle to physical diseases like cancer. Both require immense courage and endurance, and both deserve our empathy, understanding, and love.

As I close this chapter, Veronique's bravery—along with the courage of the other warriors I have shared about, and those we have lost to the battle—serves as a powerful reminder of an essential truth: those who fight for life, whether they win or lose that fight, are true warriors. Their struggle is not a sign of weakness but a testament to profound strength.

It is our collective responsibility to create a world where those battling the darkness feel seen, supported, and valued, and where their stories are met with love, compassion, and grace. Together, we can honor their resilience and help illuminate the path toward healing and hope.

PART 3

EXPLORING YOUR CAVE

Chapter 9

THE TURN
IN YOUR CAVE

Everyone has a story, and each of us carries chapters filled with pain and struggle. The good news is that, just as my pain has led to transformation and purpose, and just as the others I've shared about have found life on the other side of their struggles, the same is possible for you.

This part of the book delves into unpacking what keeps us stuck—the lies and illusions that trap us in darkness—and explores how to step into the truth. You'll see that change is not only possible but your cave can also transform into a place of light and purpose.

This is where the work begins, and I will guide you through exploring your own cave. Together, we'll uncover your path to healing and growth.

As you've read the stories of others—stories of struggle and transformation—you may have found pieces of yourself reflected in them: the pain, the questions, the darkness, and perhaps even glimpses of hope. These stories aren't just about others; they're an invitation for you to explore your own journey.

Maybe you're in the middle of your cave right now, surrounded by shadows, searching for a way out. Perhaps someone you love is lost in their own cave, and you carry the weight of their darkness. Maybe you've just started to notice the faint edges of light peeking through, or you've already emerged but still bear the weight of what you endured deep within.

Wherever you are, know this: your story matters. It's part of a greater narrative—one with the power to inspire, heal, and transform not only your life but the lives of others as well.

THE NATURE OF YOUR CAVE

Take a moment to reflect: What does your cave look like? Is it filled with grief, addiction, shame, loneliness, or hopelessness? Or is there perhaps a quiet sense of discontent—a feeling that you're merely existing rather than truly living? Maybe your struggle comes from loving someone who battles addiction and suicidality. Or perhaps it's something else entirely—a unique combination of challenges and pain that only you can fully understand.

Whatever your cave is, it's not a life sentence. It's just a chapter, not the whole book. And just as the caves in the stories you've read eventually lead to light, so can yours.

Even in my own cave of grief and darkness—one marked by losses that felt so final—there has been purpose. Through those losses, light has emerged, illuminating my path in ways I never expected. That doesn't mean there aren't dark and difficult days; there always will be. But I've learned to face each day with hope: hope that those I've lost are still with me in this fight, and hope that the life I desire is possible, even amid the pain.

STEPPING BACK TO SEE THE BIGGER PICTURE

Imagine you're standing too close to a painting, your nose almost touching the canvas. All you can see are the messy brushstrokes, smudges, and imperfections, and it's easy to believe the entire painting is flawed. But when you take a step back, the bigger picture comes into view. Suddenly, what seemed like chaos up close becomes part of a beautiful masterpiece, with each stroke contributing to the whole. Viewing your story with compassion is like stepping back from the canvas of your life. It allows you to see the beauty and purpose in the mess and appreciate how each moment, even the painful ones, fits into a larger, meaningful narrative.

The first step toward transformation is to step back and view your story with compassion. Too often, we are our own harshest critics, convinced that our struggles define us. Or we're consumed by the pain others have inflicted on us. But what if you approached your story with the same empathy you'd offer a close friend? What if, instead of judgment, you approached yourself and others with grace and curiosity?

NOTE: Journal prompts can be a powerful tool for identifying struggles and creating shifts in patterns and thinking. In the next several chapters, you'll find many prompts designed to support your healing journey. I encourage you to take out a journal or notebook to reflect on these prompts as you go, though you're welcome to revisit them later. Additionally, at the end of the book, you'll find a QR code to download the accompanying workbook, allowing you to return to the prompts whenever you're ready.

Zooming Out

- If you were to step back and view your life as a painting, what patterns or themes would emerge?

- What parts of your story feel chaotic or flawed up close but might contribute to a bigger, more beautiful picture from a wider perspective?

Compassionate Reflection

- Imagine you were speaking to a close friend who has lived your story. What words of encouragement, understanding, or compassion would you offer?

- What areas of your life have you been judging harshly? How might those experiences look if you approached them with curiosity and grace instead?

- How might the "imperfections" or "messy brushstrokes" in your painting actually add depth, character, or beauty to the overall masterpiece?

THE POWER OF STORYTELLING

Storytelling is woven into the fabric of this book for a reason: stories connect us. They remind us that we're not alone, that others have walked through darkness and found their way to the light. Just as you may have been moved by the stories in this book, your story holds the same potential to inspire.

What parts of your story are waiting to be told? What chapters of pain could become chapters of purpose? If you feel ready, begin to write—or simply imagine—the story of your cave and how it might turn toward the light. There is someone out there who needs to hear your story.

- I invite you to take some time to reflect, and write your story now.

A NEW CHAPTER AWAITS

No matter how dark your cave feels right now, you are not stuck. You are capable of change, growth, and transformation—and so is your loved one. It won't happen overnight, and the road ahead may take time, but you can get there. Your struggles do not define you. Instead, if you allow them to, they can shape you, refine you, and reveal the strength that has been within you all along.

HOW YOUR CAVE CAN TURN WHEN SUPPORTING A LOVED ONE

When supporting a loved one in their battle, setting boundaries is essential. There's a fine line between helping and enabling, and it's important to navigate with care. Always lead with love in your interactions and intentions while also maintaining clear boundaries. Both can coexist. For example, you might say:

"I am here for you, I love you, and I want nothing more than to help you when you're ready for that help. Until then, I need to [state your boundaries]."

The best thing we can do for a loved one is offer support and love while placing our focus on what we *can* control. As much as we may want to change hard things or prevent them from happening to those we love, we have come to learn through these pages that we do not ultimately control their choices; we can only influence. What you do have control over is how you respond—what you say, what you do, and how you show up in their life. The rest is up to them.

This journey is about turning inward and finding that place of peace within yourself. By doing so, you not only support them from a healthier place but you also create the space for your own healing and growth.

- I invite you to create three columns in your journal and reflect:
    - First column: When my loved one________________
    - Second column: I do not have control over______________
    - Third column: What I can control or do is____________

As I shared previously, the summer that Alex's life took a drastic turn, I felt physically ill from the weight of his choices and the path he was walking. I so badly wanted to change it. But turning inward, focusing on what I could control, and surrendering the rest was truly life-changing for me.

I realized I was allowing Alex's choices—things far beyond my control—to destroy my inner peace. The harder I tried to control what I couldn't, the more miserable and defeated I became. That moment of surrender changed everything. I shifted my focus to what I could control: how I handled my interactions with him, what I said and did, and setting boundaries with love.

While the situation itself didn't change, something within me did. I found an unshakable peace and acceptance. I came to understand that Alex's story was his own. My role was to love him, guide him, and do everything I could to help, but I couldn't carry the weight of his choices. By focusing on what I could control and letting go of the rest, I found a sense of peace that sustained me.

In this next chapter, we are going to explore the miracle mashers that keep people stuck in pain and darkness and explore how we can dismantle these illusions and step into truth, leading us to the life we desire.

Chapter 10

MIRACLE MASHERS: UNDERSTANDING THE PATTERNS THAT KEEP US STUCK

Suicidal ideation, substance use, and other struggles we face as humans are often mistaken as *the problem itself*, but in reality, these are *symptoms* of something deeper. Beneath the surface lies unresolved pain, unmet needs, and disconnection from self, others, and the Divine. To truly heal, we must look beyond the surface and address the root causes of hopelessness—what I call the *Miracle Mashers*. These internal and external forces obscure your light, trap you in despair, and keep you from stepping into the miracle of who you truly are.

As previously discussed, the core of suicidal ideation and substance use is a desire for escape. When life feels unbearably heavy, overwhelming, and impossible to navigate, the mind seeks relief. This psychological and emotional pain often arises from life's inevitable challenges—loss, trauma, disappointment, and hardship. Left unaddressed, these experiences create a mind and soul in *dis-ease*, manifesting in struggles with depression, anxiety, addiction, or hopelessness.

Depression, for instance, can be seen as the soul's cry for deep rest. But rather than seeing this as a cry for transformation, we often interpret it as hopelessness and sometimes the end of the road. This is the great illusion. Depression, anxiety, and emotional overwhelm are signals, not conclusions. They tell us that something within needs to shift.

Unfortunately, these signals are often misunderstood. Instead of responding with curiosity or compassion, we judge ourselves. We feel weak, broken, and incapable, and this self-judgment creates stuck energy—a force that poisons the mind, body, and soul. It is within this stuck energy that the Miracle Mashers take root.

Throughout my journey, I've met many people who struggle with chronic suicidal ideation. Suicidal ideation can become an ingrained pattern.

We all carry patterns, some that serve us and others that hold us back. Sometimes, we sabotage ourselves with self-doubt before we even begin something new. We may find ourselves stuck in cycles of unhealthy relationships, replaying old wounds and fears. For some, it's turning to substances or distractions to numb the pain instead of confronting it. Overworking, procrastinating, or people-pleasing can also become deeply ingrained habits. Even our thought patterns, like expecting the worst or believing we are unworthy, can form repetitive loops that keep us trapped.

When left unaddressed, these patterns shape our lives, making it feel impossible to break free. But the key is learning to pause when suicidal thoughts arise and recognize them for what they are—a pattern, not a truth. This moment of awareness is an invitation to shift. Instead of automatically reaching for the familiar escape (or eject button), I encourage you to rewire your brain to hit the **pause** button. In that pause lies the opportunity to shift—not just your mind but your entire state of being.

The good news is that these patterns and destructive forces (Miracles Mashers) are not the truth of who you are or who your loved one is. They are habits and illusions that can be dismantled.

Life often feels like a maze of distorted mirrors, each one reflecting false versions of ourselves—illusions of unworthiness, brokenness, and lack. But beyond the illusions lies the truth: **you are whole, worthy, and connected to something greater.**

What seems like an impenetrable wall of despair is often just a thin membrane that you can cut through by recognizing and embracing the truth.

- **Before the breakthrough:**
  This is the worst. I can't do this. I need to escape. Hopelessness feels like a dead-end.

- **After the breakthrough:**
  This is hard, AND I am strong enough to grow through it. You realize that struggles are not the end; they are invitations to grow into your fullest self.

As you read in the earlier chapters, the cave can turn. Pain can transform into purpose, and despair can shift into hope. But to move forward, we must first name the forces that hold us back.

In the next few chapters, we'll examine the most common Miracle Mashers—the illusions and lies that keep us stuck—that I've encountered in my years of sitting with individuals battling suicidal thoughts, addiction, and deep despair, and we'll explore how to dismantle their hold on our lives. By shining a light on these forces, you will learn how to shift from this place of hopelessness, unworthiness, and lack into a life of abundance. Through this process, you'll uncover your truth, come into wholeness, and step into a life filled with purpose and freedom.

Chapter 11

MIRACLE MASHER #1: I DON'T BELONG

One of the most pervasive lies we face is the belief that we are alone, no one cares, and that we don't belong. This illusion whispers cruel falsehoods:

You're unworthy of love.

You're an outsider in your own life.

The world would be better off without you.

You have no one.

No one cares about you.

The feelings of loneliness and not belonging stem from the false idea that something is fundamentally wrong with us.

But here's the truth: **you are not alone, and you do belong.** You were created with purpose, and your existence is part of a larger, interconnected whole. The feelings of loneliness and not belonging are just illusions born from disconnection—disconnection from yourself (your truth), from others, and from the Divine.

The illusion of loneliness stems either from the idea that we are incomplete or from the ache that comes from lack of love, acceptance, or the feeling that we are truly *seen* and *known*. This sense of emptiness creates a deep void within us, one we instinctively try to fill. In response, we often seek external validation—chasing achievements, job titles, or relationships—to belong. We look for love in all the wrong places, running toward anything that promises to make us feel loved, worthy, and complete.

Yet, when these external sources inevitably fall short of meeting our deepest needs, the void remains, and we're left feeling even more isolated and empty. The truth is, no external achievement or relationship can fully satisfy the innate longing within us.

I recently heard something powerful in a sermon by Pastor Chad Moore of Sun Valley Community Church, that spoke directly to this universal yearning: **"Everybody wants a blessing from a greater somebody."** These words resonated deeply because they reflect a fundamental truth: we all long for the blessing to be seen, to belong, to be loved, and to feel significant and valued by something—or someone—greater than ourselves.

This longing is fundamental to our human existence. The challenge is that we often search for the blessing in all the wrong places, only to find that these sources are incapable of filling the void in our hearts. The truth is, the blessing we seek cannot be fully met by anything external. The deepest and most transformative blessing comes from our higher self and higher power. For me, that is God.

Only when you accept this truth can you experience the love, belonging, and significance that no external source can provide.

The love and sense of belonging we long for have been present all along, placed within us by the One who created us. When we turn to God *and* inward—reconnecting with the divine spark within us—we begin to experience the profound truth that we are already whole, already loved, already blessed.

This shift—from seeking the blessing outside of yourself to finding it in your connection with God and your soul—is liberating. It allows you to stop striving and start living authentically, knowing that you are already enough, in and through the eyes of the Divine. The blessing is not something you earn; it's something you awaken to, a truth that has always been there.

This realization doesn't diminish the value of love or connection with others—it enhances it. When you stop seeking validation and worthiness in external sources, you can approach relationships, work, and life with a sense of fullness rather than coming from a place of need or lack. You can give and receive love freely because you understand that the blessing you long for is already within you.

For those of you walking alongside a loved one in this fight, *I see you.* I remember the loneliness I felt during the struggles we faced with Alex. It was so strange because, on one hand, I was helping kids and families navigate challenges similar to my own—I *knew* I wasn't alone. Yet, there I stood, feeling utterly isolated. I remember thinking, *How can I help others if I can't even help my own son?*

At the root of that loneliness were feelings of inadequacy as a mother and the belief that no one could truly understand my situation. I was longing for the blessing externally: to be *seen by others and to be loved by my son,* and it was only fulfilled when I turned to God and inward.

When I began to surrender to the Divine and consistently seek God's love, support, and guidance—letting go of my own understanding—everything transformed. That doesn't mean I don't struggle or still get caught up in the human tendency to seek external validation. Surrender is a daily choice, one I strive to make with intention but inevitably struggle and fail to do at times. The key is self-awareness and continually trying again. Each day, I do my best to remain aware of the need to surrender and to seek God in all I do and in every circumstance of my life. This shift is both life-giving and life-changing.

INTEGRATING ADLERIAN PSYCHOLOGY: THE IMPORTANCE OF BELONGING AND SIGNIFICANCE

To emphasize the importance of belonging and its significance to the well-being of humanity, I want to highlight Adlerian psychology, developed by Alfred Adler. Adler emphasized that belonging is an innate human need, foundational to mental and emotional health. According to Adler, a lack of these core needs often drives feelings of isolation, despair, and unworthiness. These feelings manifest as *the illusion of not belonging.* Adler's framework provides a powerful lens for understanding and dismantling this illusion while offering actionable steps to cultivate genuine belonging and significance in your life.

The Illusion of Not Belonging, Through Adler's Lens

Adler believed that every person is motivated by a desire to belong and contribute meaningfully to their community. When these needs are unmet, individuals may feel disconnected and unworthy, leading them to a sense of isolation and internal conflict. In Adlerian terms, this is often rooted in *inferiority complexes*—beliefs that we are fundamentally inadequate compared to others. These beliefs arise from early experiences, societal expectations, or distorted comparisons and can trap us in cycles of loneliness and despair. Adlerian psychology aligns seamlessly with the concept of Miracle Mashers, as both highlight the internal and external forces that obscure our innate light and keep us trapped in cycles of pain.

The good news is, these are feelings and not permanent truths; they are beliefs, and beliefs can be changed. Adler asserted that belonging is not about being perfect or earning approval; it's about cultivating connections and finding meaning through contribution and shared humanity.

Adler's framework not only explains why these illusions take root but also offers actionable steps to reclaim a sense of purpose and connection. Through cultivating belonging and significance, you can dismantle these destructive patterns and step into the truth of who you are—a miracle, whole and worthy.

Reconnecting with Significance and Belonging

Adlerian psychology teaches that the path to overcoming feelings of not belonging is twofold:

1. reconnecting with yourself (and I would add your higher power) and affirming your intrinsic value, and

2. building authentic relationships and contributing to the greater good.

Below are practical steps inspired by Adlerian principles to help you rediscover your sense of significance and belonging. Again, I invite you to get out your journal, or come back to the journal prompts via the QR code that's at the end of this book that will take you to the workbook.

HOW TO CULTIVATE BELONGING

Rebuilding the Connection to Yourself

Acknowledge Where You Are

You may feel disconnected, unworthy, or like you don't belong. That's okay. You are not alone in feeling this way. Right now, just take a breath and acknowledge what you're feeling without judgment.

- What words would you use to describe how you feel about yourself today?

- If you could say one honest sentence about your pain, what would it be?

- Where do you feel this pain in your body?

Gently Question the Lies

Sometimes, the mind tells us stories that aren't true, especially when we are in pain. The belief that you don't belong or aren't worthy may feel real, but is it possible that this belief isn't the full truth?

- Have there been even small moments in your life when you felt seen, accepted, or valued—even for a second? Write them down.

- If someone you loved felt the way you do now, what would you want to tell them?

Experiment with Self-Kindness

You don't have to believe in affirmations yet. Instead, try writing a sentence that is *neutral* and not painful—something that doesn't hurt to say, even if you're unsure if it's true.

Example:

- "I exist, and that means something."

- "Maybe I am more than my pain."

- "I don't have to have all the answers today."

Write your own version (here or in your own journal):

- ____

Even if you don't believe it yet, that's okay. Just let it exist on the page.

A Small Step Toward Connection

Belonging starts with noticing yourself again. Today, find *one small thing* that connects you to life.

Examples:

- the way the sunlight feels on your skin

- a song that stirs something in you

- a memory of a time when you felt a little bit okay

- hope through someone else's sharing of their story

Write about it here (or in your own journal):

- ______________________________________

Even if you don't believe you belong, you are here. You are reading this. That means there is still a possibility for something different. And that is enough for today.

Examine Your Beliefs

Identify and challenge beliefs that fuel feelings of disconnection or unworthiness. Write down these beliefs in your journal or the downloadable workbook, and examine their origins.

Belief: What is(are) the belief(s) you hold?

Examples:

- "I'm not lovable."

- "I'm not good enough."

- "There is something wrong with me."

Origin of Belief: Where does the belief(s) come from?

- **Example:** Parents often critiqued what I did, so I never felt good enough.

Challenge the belief.

- Identify evidence for and against the belief.
  - **Example:** Evidence that proves I am not good enough: I've made so many mistakes and ruined relationships.
- Identify alternative interpretations (consider other possible explanations).
  - Ask questions like: Is this always true? What evidence do I have that contradicts this belief?
  - **Example:** Evidence that proves I AM good enough.
    - Mistakes are a part of being human, and every experience has taught me something.
    - My worth is not tied to my mistakes.
    - While some relationships may have been hurt, I have the ability to grow, make amends, and build healthier connections moving forward.

Challenge the Illusion of Isolation

Recognize that everyone shares struggles, fears, and hopes.

- Write down three ways you are connected to others—shared experiences, goals, or emotions. You can identify stories of others, whether in this book or along your path, that you have connected with (even if you don't personally know the person).

Redefine Success

Reflect on how you define success and challenge societal norms (reflect on how you may be conforming to the patterns of the world). Shift your focus from external validation to intrinsic values like kindness, resilience, and integrity.

- How do you define success?

- What positive traits and qualities do you possess or want to work toward possessing? List them here (or in your journal) and also display them in a visible place.

Practice Self-compassion

Treat yourself with kindness, especially when self-doubt arises. Remind yourself that everyone experiences struggle.

- How can you be more kind and gentle with yourself?

Cultivate Joy in Solitude

Spend time with yourself doing activities you love—walking in nature, journaling, or pursuing hobbies. Differentiate between *loneliness* and *solitude*. Connection with yourself happens in the quiet moments.

- What brings you joy?

Note: Be intentional about making time for these things regularly.

Reconnecting with the Divine

Belonging is deeply rooted in your relationship with God, the Universe, or the Divine. Spend time in prayer, meditation, or reflection.

- Affirm your connection: I am a child of the Creator. I am whole, loved, and belong to something greater than myself.

- Pray, meditate, spend time in nature, or read spiritual texts to nurture this connection.

  - List the ways that feel right for you to begin to create connection with your higher power.

BUILD AUTHENTIC CONNECTIONS: CONTRIBUTE TO THE GREATER GOOD

Take initiative in relationships.

Share your thoughts or feelings with someone you trust. Vulnerability fosters intimacy and connection.

- Who could you reach out to? What is important for you to share?

Shift focus from belonging to contribution.

Strengthen your sense of belonging by helping others. Embrace the Adlerian principle that your well-being is tied to the well-being of others. Cultivate empathy by listening to someone else's story or participating in acts of service. **Reframe the question "Do I belong here?" to "How can I contribute here?" Contribution reinforces connection and dissolves feelings of isolation.**

- Ask yourself: How can I use my gifts and skills to contribute to others?
  - Look for opportunities to serve others, even in small ways—a kind word, a thoughtful text, or a smile can create a ripple effect.
- Ask yourself: How can I contribute today?

Join a community.

We are not meant to do life alone. Seek spaces where you feel aligned, such as interest-based groups, faith communities, or support networks. Shared goals create connection and reduce isolation.

- What communities interest you? Once you identify this, the key is to take action and join a group or community that aligns with your values.

Celebrate the shared human experience.

Reflect on how your struggles have made you or could make you more empathetic and open to others. Recognizing that everyone carries their own battles fosters compassion and connection.

Create meaning in what you do each day.

- Reflect on how your daily tasks, no matter how small they may seem, contribute to something greater.

- Or, reflect on what shifts you want to make in your day-to-day to begin to create meaning. Again, they can be small shifts.

By contributing to the greater good, you reaffirm your belonging in the interconnected fabric of life.

ALIGN WITH THE DIVINE IN RELATIONSHIPS AND CONTRIBUTION

Adler's principles teach us that life is rooted in connection. The sense of not belonging may feel overwhelming, but it is merely a perception, not a reality. True belonging begins when you recognize that you are already worthy simply because you exist. By deepening your connection with God, embracing the truth of who you are, cultivating authentic relationships, and contributing to the greater good, you can dismantle this illusion and step into the miracle of your significance.

Focus less on what you accomplish and more on who you are becoming **because who you are matters far more than any achievement.** As you engage in relationships and serve others, remember that these actions are not just about external connection; they are reflections of the divine essence within you. Every act of kindness, every moment of vulnerability, is an opportunity to embody the love and belonging that has always been yours.

Chapter 12

MIRACLE MASHER #2: I AM NOT WORTHY

One of the most harmful illusions we face is the belief that we are "not enough" or "not worthy," which leaves us in a state of lack. This lie traps us in a relentless cycle of striving to prove our worth, leaving us exhausted and unfulfilled. Alternatively, we may succumb to the belief entirely, giving up on our hopes and dreams before they even have a chance to take root. The result is a spiral of comparison, inadequacy, and self-doubt that makes it nearly impossible to feel whole. We become victims to fear, paralyzed and unable to step into all the potential that lies inside of us.

But here's the truth: **You are enough. You always have been.** Worthiness is not something you earn; it is an intrinsic part of who you are. Like the illusion of not belonging, the illusion of "not being enough" arises when we measure ourselves against external factors—achievements, possessions, or the approval of others. These comparisons disconnect us from the inherent truth of our value. However, true worth has nothing to do with these external markers. It is already within you, long before you accomplish anything or gain anyone's validation.

For those supporting a loved one battling addiction or suicidality, this illusion of "not enough" often takes on an even heavier weight. Watching someone you love struggle so deeply can lead to self-blame and feelings of inadequacy. You might think, *If I were a better parent, partner, or friend, they wouldn't be suffering like this.* It's easy to fall into the trap of comparison—looking at others' lives and wondering why this pain has come to your family—or feeling like you're failing your loved one in some way. But just as your loved one's worth is not defined by their struggle, your worth is not defined by your ability to save or fix them. Their journey is their own.

SIGNIFICANCE: OVERCOMING THE ILLUSION OF NOT BEING ENOUGH

In Adlerian psychology, significance means recognizing that your life has value and purpose. The illusion of not being enough, fueled by societal pressures, internalized false beliefs, and constant comparison undermines this truth. When you feel insignificant, you might chase external validation or avoid pursuing your purpose altogether, fearing failure or rejection.

To overcome this illusion, Adler emphasized the importance of reconnecting with your intrinsic worth and finding meaning through contribution. **Significance is not achieved by what you have or what others think of you; it arises from knowing that your life matters and that your presence—the way you show up in the world—makes a difference.**

PRACTICAL STEPS TO RECLAIM YOUR WORTHINESS AND SIGNIFICANCE

Affirm Your Inherent Worth and Shift Your Internal Narrative

Life-giving statements

Although this may sound basic, what we tell ourselves is powerful. Therefore, we must speak life-giving words to ourselves every single day. Start each day by repeating life-giving statements like:

- *I am enough, just as I am.*
- *My significance is inherent and not tied to what I do or achieve.*
- *My mistakes (or past) do not define me.*
- *I am loveable just as I am.*

What are your life-giving statements?

- Write these statements down where you can see them often to serve as a constant reminder of your truth.

Turn Inward

When the illusion of lack creeps in, pause and ask yourself, *Am I seeking external approval or validation?* Use this as a cue to shift your focus inward, reminding yourself that worthiness begins within.

Journal Prompt: Focus on what is within your control—your actions, words, and behaviors.

What is within my control each day?

- *Ask yourself: How can I act in ways that align with my values?* By living in alignment with your core values, you naturally strengthen your sense of inherent worth. You can start with these 4 categories:

What do you value or what is important to you when it comes to

1. relationships,
2. work/education,
3. leisure,
4. personal development, health, and spirituality?

Note: When life throws you a curveball or you face hard things day-to-day, the point is to focus on your valued direction. Think about what really matters to you and commit to having your daily actions align with your values.

EMBRACE SELF-FORGIVENESS

Carrying guilt or shame makes it hard to feel worthy. If this resonates with you, you're not alone—and you're in the right place.

Guilt and shame weigh heavily on the heart, creating walls between us and our growth. I've been there, stuck in cycles of regret and self-blame, paralyzed by past mistakes. But here's the truth: holding onto these emotions doesn't serve you. It keeps you anchored in pain, blocking your path to healing.

Self-forgiveness isn't about excusing mistakes or wrongdoings. It's about releasing the grip of the past so you can move forward. A concept that changed my life—rooted in evidence-based practices like Dialectical Behavioral Therapy (DBT)—is this: we're all doing the best we can with the knowledge, tools, and experiences we have. This doesn't justify harmful actions, but it acknowledges the context in which they happened. The hope is that as we learn better, we do better.

I used this truth to forgive myself for mistakes I made in my parenting. My intentions were rooted in love, but I still stumbled. Recognizing that I did my best with what I knew allowed me to extend grace to myself—and grace is essential. Without it, we risk carrying bitterness and staying stuck. Grace opens the door to forgiveness, helping us release the past and step into the present with love.

Forgiveness—whether for yourself or others—doesn't condone behavior. It frees your heart from guilt, shame, and resentment so you can live fully. Mistakes are part of being human; they're how we learn and grow.

Let's walk through some simple but powerful journal prompts to help you release guilt and embrace the miracle of who you are.

Acknowledge the Weight

Without judgment, name what you feel.

- What guilt or shame are you holding on to?

- Where do you feel it in your body?

- How has it impacted your life, relationships, or growth?

Separate Actions from Identity

Your mistakes do not define you.

- Write about your mistakes (or guilt/shame) objectively—what happened—without labeling yourself as "bad" or "unworthy."

Find the Lessons

Mistakes teach us.

- What have you learned from this?

- How can you grow from it?

- What steps will help prevent you from repeating the same mistakes?

Offer Yourself Compassion

Treat yourself as you would a loved one.

- Write a letter to yourself as if you were writing to someone you care about, offering kindness and understanding.

Release the Burden

Letting go is a conscious act.

- Write: "I forgive myself for [specific action]. I acknowledge my humanity and choose to let this go to create space for healing."

- Perform a symbolic act, like tearing up the page or visualizing the weight lifting from you.

Reaffirm Your Worth

You are not your mistakes; you are a miracle.

- Affirm:

    - I am worthy of love and forgiveness.
    - My past does not define me; I am choosing to focus on my choices today.
    - I choose love and release guilt.

Make Amends (if applicable)

If you've harmed others, making amends can heal both sides.

- Can you apologize or repair the harm?
  - Even if you can't personally apologize to the person, apologize in your heart or through writing.
- How can you move forward with integrity?

Create a Forgiveness Ritual

Mark this shift with a meaningful ritual.

- Meditate, visualizing light filling the heavy spaces.
- Write a letter to your past self offering grace.
- Plant a seed to symbolize new beginnings.

Commit to Moving Forward

Embrace the freedom of forgiveness.

- What steps will you take to honor yourself moving forward?
- How will you treat yourself with compassion when self-doubt arises?

EMBRACE A GROWTH MINDSET

Rather than seeing your pain and challenges as proof of inadequacy, view them as opportunities for growth. Ask yourself:

- What can I learn from this?
- How can this experience help me grow into the person I am meant to be?
- Celebrate small victories along the way to reinforce your sense of accomplishment and significance. Write down some of your small victories. It could be as simple as "I got out of bed today."

REFRAME YOUR PERSPECTIVE ON ABUNDANCE

Mindset is a powerful tool for dismantling the illusion of lack. When you shift your focus from lack to abundance, you begin to see yourself as whole, worthy, and complete. Gratitude amplifies this transformation, as it aligns your heart and mind with the truth of what you already have.

Never underestimate the power of gratitude: cultivate a gratitude practice by listing three things you're grateful for each day, no matter how big or small. Gratitude works like a lens that reframes your life, redirecting your focus from what you feel is missing to the abundance already present.

Recommended resource: *The Magic* by Rhonda Byrne, is an inspiring book and guide to cultivating a gratitude mindset in your daily life. This book provides practical tools and life-changing insights that help you reframe every experience—even life's challenges—through the alchemy of gratitude. It's a refreshing, transformational perspective of the magic that gratitude can have on our lives.

Write about What You Are Grateful For

Remember, it could be very simple things; every little thing matters—nothing is too small.

Visualize Abundance

Take a moment to close your eyes and **envision what it would feel like to be enough and worthy** just as you are.

Then envision what your life would look like if it was filled with love, potential, and purpose.

- *What are you doing?*

- *What do you see?*

- *How do you feel?*

Imagine letting go of whatever burdens you are carrying and moving through life lighter and proud. **Allow this vision to remind you** that you already have this love, potential, and purpose inside of you; you lack nothing. **Thank your past self** for the lessons learned, **honor your present self** for stepping into healing, and **envision your future self** living the life you desire, knowing that each step of the way you are exactly where you need to be and who you need to be to grow your soul. *Your past, present, and future self holds everything you need for this journey called life.*

Remember, **lack cannot thrive in a heart filled with gratitude and abundance.** Gratitude pulls you out of the state of lack and anchors you in abundance.

CHAPTER REFLECTION

By taking part in these reflections and practicing these steps, you can begin to dismantle the illusion of lack and reconnect with your inherent worth and significance. Remember, worthiness is not something to earn—it is already within you. Our mistakes do not define us; they exist to teach us. Through gratitude and perspective shifts, you will discover that the abundance you seek has always been there, waiting for you to embrace it.

For those supporting a loved one who is struggling, I want to reiterate how easy it is to get caught in the cycle of comparison. You might find yourself asking, *Why is this happening to me or my family?* Or you may feel inadequate as a parent, partner, or supporter. These feelings of "not enough" can creep in, fueled by the challenges of watching someone you love battle addiction or suicidality.

It's important to remember that your worth is not defined by your ability to fix their struggle. Their pain is not a reflection of your value or love. The same illusion of lack that we work to dismantle within ourselves also plays a role in their journey; feelings of unworthiness often lie at the heart of addiction and suicidality. As you reconnect with your own worth and seek peace within, you also create a foundation of stability and love that can inspire and support them in their healing journey when they are ready.

Be gentle with yourself. Acknowledge the immense strength it takes to stand beside someone in their pain while also choosing to anchor yourself in hope and self-compassion. Your love matters, your efforts matter, and most importantly—you matter.

Chapter 13

MIRACLE MASHER #3: THIS PAIN WILL NEVER END

Pain is an inevitable part of life, but our resistance to it often creates more suffering than the pain itself. We avoid it, suppress it, or numb it, convinced it has no place in a meaningful life. But what if pain isn't the enemy? What if, instead of resisting it, you leaned into pain as a teacher—a catalyst for growth?

Adler taught that pain and struggle are natural parts of life and essential for growth. Rather than avoiding or numbing pain, he encouraged embracing it as an opportunity to develop courage, resilience, and empathy.

In my life, psychological pain has been one of my greatest teachers. It was when I dropped to my knees that I learned how to rise. When my heart broke, my soul expanded. So often, we view pain, heartbreak, and immense struggles as the end of the road—but that's an illusion meant to keep us stuck. The truth is, pain holds profound lessons if we have the courage to face it.

Through my most painful experiences, I've discovered that pain is not a punishment but an opportunity—a chance to grow and transform in ways I never imagined. Those painful moments shaped the person I am today.

When we embrace pain, it becomes a guide, uncovering the parts of our lives that long for healing and transformation. It holds the potential to propel us forward, if we allow it to move through us. Avoiding pain only keeps it trapped, but by approaching it with curiosity and courage, we create space for deep healing and meaningful growth.

Think of mental pain like the physical pain and soreness after a workout: it's uncomfortable, but it also indicates expansion and progress. Similarly, emotional pain is not a barrier but a bridge—an invitation to pause, reflect, and let go of what no longer serves us. It offers a chance to step back and examine the patterns, beliefs, or attachments that keep us stuck and confront the truths we might otherwise avoid. When embraced, it becomes a powerful pathway to transformation and renewal. By shifting our perspective, pain ceases to be an obstacle and instead becomes an opportunity to heal, grow, and rewrite our story.

During my prayer time one day, a five-step process was revealed to me—one that became transformative in my own healing journey. As I applied it to my deepest pain points, its impact was undeniable. Over time, this process evolved into what I now call the *Rise and Rewrite Process*—a powerful tool designed to help you transform your pain and rewrite your story.

We often forget that we hold the key to our own story. While we may not always have control of what happens to us, we do have a say in how we interpret our experiences and the narrative we create from our experiences—both the painful and the beautiful.

This framework gently guides you through discomfort, uncovering the narratives and illusions within your pain. By revealing the truth, you are empowered to transform suffering into strength and renewal. Pain may shape us, but it does not have to define us.

Too often, we let our past dictate who we are, forgetting that we hold the pen to write and re-write our own story. Through this process, you'll learn to embrace truth, release the weight of the past, and step into a more empowered version of yourself. Together, we'll create a story of growth, resilience, and renewal.

Again, I would invite you to get out a journal or notebook. For this process, I encourage you to take the time to do it now, but of course you may come back to it.

THE RISE AND REWRITE PROCESS

Pain is not just something to endure—it's a messenger. It carries wisdom, showing us what needs healing, what's out of alignment, and what we're being called to release. This process will help you engage with your pain in a transformative way, to shift from suffering to empowerment.

Step One: Identify the Point of Pain

Instead of resisting pain, approach it with **curiosity**. What is it trying to tell you?

Reflect:

- What is my point of pain? What is causing me distress?

- Where do I feel this pain in my body?

- What emotions arise when I sit with this pain?

Step Two: Unveil the Storyline

We all create narratives around our pain—some consciously, some unconsciously. These storylines shape how we see ourselves and the world. But are they true?

Common storylines we create around pain and suffering include:

- **Personal failure**: "I failed because I wasn't good enough, smart enough, or strong enough." "This wouldn't have happened if I had tried harder or been more capable."

- **Unworthiness**: "I deserve this pain because I'm not worthy of love, success, or happiness." "This happened because something is wrong with me."

- **Betrayal:** "I can't trust anyone because people will always hurt or abandon me." "This person's actions prove that I'm unlovable or unimportant."

- **Loss**: "I've lost my chance at happiness, and nothing will ever be the same." "This pain (or loss) has taken away my ability to live a fulfilling life."

- **Victimhood**: "The world is against me, and I have no control over what happens." "Bad things always happen to me."

- **Shame**: "If people knew what happened, they'd think less of me." "This pain defines who I am—it's a reflection of my worth."

- **Permanence**: "This pain will never go away; I'll always feel like this." "My life is permanently damaged because of this experience."

- **Injustice**: "This shouldn't have happened to me; it's unfair, and I can't move on." "Life isn't fair, and I'm stuck because of someone else's choices."

    - I want to acknowledge here that some pain is undeniably unjust, and acknowledging that truth is vital. However, healing begins when we recognize that while we **can't change what happened to us, we can reclaim our power**. Both truths can coexist. Example: "What happened to me was wrong, AND I still have the power to move forward."

- **Isolation**: "No one else understands what I'm going through." "I'm all alone in this, and I can't rely on anyone."

- **Identity**: "This pain is who I am; it defines me and my life." "I'll never be more than this broken version of myself."

Reflect

- What storyline have I created around this pain?

- What has this pain taken from me (if applicable)?

- How has this narrative shaped my identity and choices?

Step Three: Identify the Illusions, Lies, and Inner Critic

Pain often amplifies our **inner critic**, feeding feelings of inadequacy and self-doubt. It may whisper false beliefs like:

- "I'm not strong enough."

- "This will never get better."

- "I'm a failure."

- "This is all my fault."

Now, **name these false beliefs**. When we bring them into the light, we weaken their hold.

Reflect:

- What is my inner critic saying?

- What illusions or lies am I believing?

By recognizing these distortions, you **create space** to challenge them and replace them with empowering truths.

Step Four: Identify the Truths

Now that you've uncovered the lies, it's time to focus on the **truth**. First, we'll explore **part mapping**, an Internal Family Systems (IFS) technique that reveals how pain stems from wounded parts of ourselves. Each part plays a role in protecting us from further harm or suffering. Though often misunderstood, these parts hold valuable insights and intentions. I encourage you to look up IFS part mapping for a deeper understanding of it.

Example:

A person struggling with deep unworthiness might uncover a wounded **childhood part** that felt invisible. When asked what it needs to hear, it may say:

"I need to know that I matter."

The person—from their wiser, more compassionate self—can then respond:

"You are seen. You are loved. You are enough—just as you are."

Reflect:

- What is the name of this wounded part?
- How old is it? (When did it first appear in my life?)
- In what ways does this part try to protect me?
- What does it need to know?
- How can I show up for it with compassion?

Practical Exercise:

Journal your responses and sit with this part, offering it reassurance. The goal is not to suppress or reject it but to acknowledge it with compassion and begin integrating it into your healing journey.

Now looking to what's **true**:

Repeat to yourself:

- I am resilient.
- Pain is a universal part of growth.
- My past does not define my future.
- I am worthy of healing and happiness.

Reflect:

- What is true about myself?

- What is true about my ability to grow through this?

- What truths do I need to hold onto daily?

Step Five: Rewrite the Story

It's time to **reclaim your power** by rewriting your story. This isn't about denying the pain but **transforming how you carry it.**

Instead of:

✕ *"This pain has ruined my life."*

☑ **"This pain has revealed my strength and led me to what truly matters."**

Instead of:

✕ *"I'm broken because of this."*

☑ **"I am learning, growing, and becoming more resilient."**

Reflect:

- How can I see this pain as part of my growth?

- What strengths or values has it revealed?

- How do I want to define my future?

Rewrite your story and place it somewhere visible. Let this be the **truth** that guides you forward.

Important note: This process can be used for **each** pain point that keeps you stuck. Healing is a journey, but **you have the power to rise and rewrite your story**—one chapter at a time.

CHAPTER REFLECTION

As we close these chapters on Miracle Mashers, let us reflect on this evident truth: belonging is not something we must earn; it is something we inherently possess. The illusions of disconnection and isolation are powerful, but they are not truths. They are narratives born from pain and fear, yet they can be dismantled through reconnection—with ourselves, our Creator, and those around us.

Your worth is intrinsic; it is rooted in who you are, pure and whole. Every single one of us is inherently whole on a soul level, something we will explore in the next chapter. Your worth is not rooted in what you do (good or bad), what you achieve or fail at, or any external forces—including how others perceive you. You are a miracle of creation, deeply loved and seen by the Divine.

Pain, though challenging, can be the fertile ground for radical transformation. Let it serve as the alchemy that helps you discover your true self and the resilience within you. This resilience can guide you to uncover the deep, abiding peace in your soul—a peace that has and always will be there, no matter what hardships life may bring.

By embracing the practices and perspectives shared here, you can begin to uncover the lies and illusions that have kept you from fully living in your truth. Step into the light of your belonging and significance, not only for yourself but also as a beacon of hope and connection for others who may be trapped in their own illusions. When we take our pain and use it to fuel our purpose—like the warriors you've read about throughout these pages—we tap into the belonging and significance that are vital to our human existence.

For those supporting a loved one who is struggling, this journey is equally yours. It can be incredibly difficult to stand alongside someone wrestling with their darkness, but your presence, compassion, and unwavering love carry immeasurable power. Remember, your worth is not defined by your ability to "fix" their struggles, nor is their pain a reflection of your value. Instead, by grounding yourself in your own truth and worth, you create a stable foundation from which you can offer meaningful support.

PART 4

THE EXIT FROM THE CAVE

Chapter 14

COMING HOME TO YOURSELF

Now that we've uncovered the forces—Miracle Mashers—that obscure our light and keep us trapped in cycles of despair, and you've had time to reflect and begin to make the necessary shifts in your life to find your way out of your cave, it's time to focus inward and upward. Beneath the layers of illusion, pain, and false beliefs lies an undeniable truth: **you are whole on a soul level.** You always have been.

Part of the human condition involves making mistakes and experiencing struggles, which can lead us to the feeling of "brokenness." But on a soul level, we are—and always have been—whole. Brokenness is a "wordly illusion," just like the other illusions we've uncovered. Once we can tap into our soul and our inherent wholeness, this sense of brokenness can begin to dissipate. From a space of truth and wholeness, we see life differently: everything and everyone is inherently good and whole.

The brokenness we perceive is a reflection of being trapped by the darkness that exists in the world and our human lives. But the truth remains: **you are not broken—you are whole.** Healing is not about fixing what's broken; it's about rediscovering the miracle that has always been within you. It's about peeling back the lies that cloud your vision and reconnecting with the truth of who you are.

SUPPORTING A LOVED ONE

As we explore the concept of wholeness, it's vital to extend this understanding to those we love, especially when they are battling the shadows of suicidal ideation or addiction. Witnessing someone you care about being in pain can be overwhelming, and the instinct to "fix" them can feel urgent. But just as healing is not about fixing what's broken, supporting a loved one isn't about saving them—it's about holding space for them to rediscover their own light.

First, recognize their inherent worth and wholeness, even if they cannot see it for themselves right now. Speak words of hope and truth into their life: remind them that they are not broken, they are loved, and their struggles do not define them. Your belief in their wholeness can serve as a lifeline in their darkest moments.

Second, be a safe and nonjudgmental presence. Validate their feelings. Sometimes, simply sitting in the silence of their struggle with them can remind them they are seen and valued.

Third, remember that you are not responsible for their healing, but you can guide them toward resources that support their journey. Encouraging professional help, such as therapy, support groups, or treatment programs, can make a profound difference. Offer to help them find those resources or accompany them if they feel afraid to take that step alone. If they are not ready for the help, this is where boundaries are of the utmost importance, particularly when supporting someone struggling with addiction, so your help does not turn into enabling. Enabling helps no one, but making it known you are there to help them when they are ready is the loving thing to do.

Finally, take care of yourself. Supporting someone through these battles can be emotionally taxing, and your own well-being is crucial. When you operate from a place of balance and self-compassion, you'll be better equipped to provide the support they need.

In this chapter, as we explore what it means to rediscover wholeness, let us hold space not only for our own journeys but also for the sacred role we can play in supporting those battling addiction or suicidality and those of us grieving someone we've lost to this battle. Together, we'll move beyond the pain that has held us back and step fully into the light of our true selves—individually and as a collective.

THE TRUTH OF YOUR EXISTENCE: YOU ARE A MIRACLE

The odds of your existence—**1 in 400 trillion**—serves as a powerful reminder that your life is no accident. You are here for a reason. You are not broken; you are **becoming.** The human experience, while often filled with challenges and illusions of incompleteness, cannot alter the essence of your soul. Your true essence is whole, and it always has been.

To illustrate this idea that we are already whole, I want to share some key concepts from *The Mel Robbins Podcast*, during which Robbins interviewed Dr. Zach Bush, a triple board-certified physician who worked with people nearing death in hospice and ICU. Bush also had his own near-death experience. The episode is titled, "Near Death Experiences: The Ultimate Truth About Your Soul's Purpose, Consciousness, & Oneness." In the podcast, Dr. Bush discussed how both his near-death experience and his work with others helped him realize that everything in life happens exactly as it should to teach us the lessons we need to learn so we become the people we are meant to be. In this process of evolving, we come to realize that we have always been whole. Any perception of incompleteness is an illusion.

Healing on a Spiritual Level

Healing isn't about fixing what's wrong but about undoing the belief that you are not whole. It's about stepping out of the state of dis-ease caused by these illusions and learning to live authentically with God at the center of life. Think about the moments in life that bring peace and clarity: watching a bird in nature, sitting by a flowing river, hiking through a forest of tall trees, watching a sunset on the beach, or staring into a newborn baby's eyes. In those moments, things just feel *right*. That's your soul recognizing its wholeness. In those moments, you feel connected to something greater. The truth is, this connection is always there—you just need to learn how to access it daily.

Journal Reflection: Moments of Connection

Think about a time you felt truly at peace or deeply connected to something greater—whether in nature, in the presence of someone you love, or during a quiet, reflective moment. What were you doing? How did it feel? Write about how these moments remind you of wholeness.

TURNING INWARD: THE PATH TO REDISCOVERING YOUR WHOLENESS

One of the most fundamental shifts we can make is learning to fill our own soul with approval, love, and acceptance. As I have continually noted throughout this book, we need to eliminate both the desire for outside approval and the measuring of our worth by external factors. True fulfillment comes from within. In an interview on Jay Shetty's podcast, *On Purpose*, country star Jelly Roll said, "We need to start with looking at the man in the mirror" (episode titled, "Jelly Roll's Brutal Journey of Self-forgiveness"). Self should always be the go-to for both reflection and approval.

Journal Reflection: The Mirror of Self

If you were to look in the mirror right now and speak to your soul, what would you say? What would it mean to truly accept and love yourself in this moment without needing external approval or validation?

We must deeply understand that we are valuable before we achieve anything or earn anyone's approval. Dr. Bush shared that "the number one regret [people express as they approach death] is 'I was performing the whole time. I never was actually being me.'" They were afraid to be themselves, didn't even know what it would feel like to be themselves. As they near the end and the veil of illusions is lifted, they are reconnected on a soul level and it is then they realize their true beauty and worth.

Dr. Bush noted that people often reflect, "If I had just known I was whole the whole time" and could have savored life for what it was, instead of constantly seeing it for what it wasn't. We spend so much energy focusing on what life *isn't* that we miss the miracle of what it *is*.

REMEMBERING WHO YOU ARE

You are a unique creation living a human life to help your soul grow. Every soul is pure and complete, but life's challenges often lead us to forget this truth. It's usually after we walk through deep difficulty and pain that we find ourselves on a journey of self-discovery, reconnecting with our soul and the Divine, and remembering our wholeness.

As Dr. Zach Bush put it at the end of his interview on Mel Robbins's podcast, "I would encourage every human to meet yourself . . . to fall deeply in love with your state as a being that is whole at every step of life and as soon as you do, we will all follow into a very beautiful reality."

You are here on purpose, with a purpose, and you are equipped with everything you need for this journey. You *have* everything you need, and you *are* everything you need.

Journal Reflection: Your Unique Purpose

Reflect on the idea that you are here on purpose, with a purpose, and are already equipped for this journey. What does this truth mean to you? How could it change the way you see your life and the challenges you've faced?

THE JOURNEY HOME TO YOURSELF

As we close this chapter on rediscovering wholeness, I invite you to take a deep breath and let these truths settle into your soul: You are not broken. You are not missing pieces. You are whole, and you always have been. The struggles, the pain, the moments of doubt—none of them define you. They are part of your human journey, not the sum of who you are.

This path of healing and self-discovery isn't about becoming someone new; it's about **remembering** who you've always been. It's about peeling back the layers of false beliefs, releasing the weight of unworthiness, and stepping fully into the miracle of your existence. You were never meant to stay in the cave. The light is always there, waiting for you to see it.

Through the stories in this book, you've witnessed transformation—proof that healing is possible, purpose can rise from pain, and hope is never out of reach. Now, the invitation is yours: **Will you choose to see yourself as whole? Will you choose to believe that you are enough just as you are?**

If nothing else stays with you from this chapter, let it be this: **You are here for a reason. Your existence is a miracle. You are enough. You are whole.** And the moment you truly embrace this truth, everything begins to change.

This is not the end of your journey—it's the beginning of seeing yourself clearly, maybe for the first time. The world needs the light only you can bring. **It's time to step forward and shine.**

Chapter 15

FROM DEATH TO LIFE

THE PERSPECTIVE SHIFT

Our perspective shapes our reality. Each of us has our own subjective truth—a unique lens through which we experience the world—shaped by our life experiences and perceptions of those experiences.

This concept reminds me of siblings—even twins—who grow up in the same home yet often turn out so differently. As a twin myself, I know firsthand how easy it is to assume that twins must be similar: same upbringing, same environment, same womb at the same time. But the truth is, my twin and I are distinct individuals, each with our own personality. We are very different in many ways, interpreting our shared childhood experiences through completely different perspectives. This illustrates how personal and unique each person's subjective truth really is.

Perspectives can shift at any given time, however. I like to think of perspective as a camera lens—when you change the lens, the way you see the world changes. This simple yet sometimes challenging adjustment has the power to transform your reality, opening the door to profound change.

I've experienced this firsthand in many areas of my life, but one of the most significant was returning to church and deepening my relationship with God. When I shifted my perspective and opened my heart, my entire reality—and the way I saw God—changed. While many factors shape who we become, the power of perspective is undeniable.

When we shift our perspective, pain and suffering no longer signify the end. Instead, they become essential components of our growth—stepping stones that lead us toward uncovering our truth. Growth is born from discomfort, and within the growth process we begin to recognize the patterns and illusions we've been holding onto that no longer serve us. Letting go of these outdated beliefs allows us to step into who we truly are and embrace our purpose.

Each of us plays a vital role in the unfolding human story. When we resist or deny our part, we inadvertently perpetuate the illusions that keep both ourselves and the world in pain. It's time to bless the past, release its grip on us, and move forward with hope and intention toward an abundant future.

True joy is found in the present moment, yet too often our souls remain dormant, distracted by the noise of our thoughts and fears tethered to the past or future. Miracles are unfolding around us every day, but we may fail to see them if we are stuck in our minds. To awaken, we must intentionally step into those deeper spiritual spaces—spaces filled with faith, love, and hope—that connect us to our essence and the Divine.

SHIFTING FROM VICTIMHOOD TO GROWTH

Changing your perspective begins with reframing your mindset. Instead of thinking, *This is happening to me,* shift to *This is happening for me.* This simple yet profound adjustment moves you from a place of victimhood—which keeps you stuck—to a place of learning and growth that propels you forward. It doesn't diminish the reality of being a victim of difficult experiences; rather, it ensures you **don't remain trapped** in that identity, which can erode your soul and prevent you from healing.

Ask yourself:

- *How can this grow me?*

- *How can I turn this pain into my purpose?*

If you've ever felt like giving up but are still here, you are a warrior. Shift your perspective from seeing yourself as unworthy or broken to recognizing the truth: *You have fought through the darkest battles and survived. You have survived your hardest day thus far.* **That makes you a warrior.** Let this truth fill every part of your being. What feels like an impenetrable wall is often just a thin membrane; you can break through and step into wholeness.

If you have feelings of inadequacy, trust this truth: **God doesn't call the qualified; He qualifies the called.** Your life has meaning, and the Divine—whether you see it as God, the Universe, or something else—will equip you with everything you need to fulfill your purpose. You are not broken. You are becoming.

TURNING ON THE LIGHT: MOVING FROM DARKNESS TO LIFE

The first step to finding light in our lives is simple: we must open our eyes and shift the lens.

One morning in my favorite place on earth—Vail, Colorado—I had an extraordinary moment during my morning prayer time. I experienced this truth in a profound and transformative way. Stepping out onto the patio, I saw the eastern sky still cloaked in darkness, with only a faint glow hinting at the rising sun. I closed my eyes, centered myself, and began my morning prayer, asking God what needed to go next in my book.

When I opened my eyes just minutes later, everything had changed. The sun had risen, flooding the mountains and trees with radiant light. It was as if the world had been transformed before my very eyes in a matter of minutes. At that moment, I heard God's whisper, "The light is always around you. Always there, waiting for you to see it. Focus your eyes on the light, and the darkness cannot persist."

This moment was a powerful reminder that darkness is not a force we must fight—it is simply the absence of light. When we focus on the light, the darkness naturally dissipates. The shadows lose their power when illuminated by truth, love, and hope.

The same is true for the darkness within us. We often try to banish it by sheer willpower, but the real transformation comes when we shine light into those hidden spaces. Light illuminates the truth, revealing that what once felt overwhelming is often less formidable when seen clearly. By turning our attention toward love, gratitude, and the presence of God, we shift our focus from what we lack to what we have—from fear to faith and from despair to hope.

To eliminate darkness in our lives, we must:

- **Acknowledge it.** Name the darkness. Whether it's fear, pain, shame, or doubt, acknowledge its presence without judgment.

- **Shine light on it.** Bring it into the open by speaking about it, praying over it, or writing it down. Light reveals truth, and truth sets us free.

- **Choose the light.** Make a conscious choice to focus on what is good, true, and beautiful. Surround yourself with positive influences, immerse yourself in gratitude, and lean into faith.

Ask yourself:

What is true, good, and beautiful (it could be as simple as "I have made it this far in this book.")?

When we choose to focus on the light, even the darkest corners of our lives begin to transform. This isn't about denying the existence of pain or challenges; it's about refusing to let them define us. The light is always there, waiting for us to open our eyes and let it in.

WHAT KEEPS US IN THE DARK

Despite the light always being present, many of us remain stuck in the dark because of patterns and beliefs that hold us back. So, what are the common patterns we get stuck in?

- **Rumination and Projection**
  - We get stuck overthinking the past or worrying about the future, robbing ourselves of the peace and beauty found in the present moment.

- **Suppressing Truth**
  - Ignoring or suppressing our emotions or reality creates inner turmoil and disconnection from our authentic selves. This often leads to depression—a "deep rest" signaling that something in our lives needs to change.

- **Pain and Trauma**
  - Unhealed pain and trauma often act as anchors tethering us to the darkness. These experiences leave wounds that, when ignored or suppressed, fester and become shame, anger, fear, or resentment. Trauma creates a distorted lens through which we view ourselves and the world, convincing us that the darkness is all there is. The weight of past hurts can feel insurmountable, keeping us from believing in the possibility of healing, light, or a brighter future.

- **Giving Away Control**
  - Allowing external circumstances or people to dictate our peace leaves us feeling powerless.

- **Resisting Surrender**
  - Holding tightly to control over things we cannot change traps us in frustration and anxiety. True freedom comes when we surrender to and trust in the Divine and the process of life.

- **Shame**
  - Shame is a heavy chain that binds us to our pain, convincing us that we are unworthy of love, healing, or a way forward. It keeps us stuck in the dark by

distorting our truth, isolating us in silence, and making us believe that our struggles define us rather than being part of our journey toward growth and light. Working through self-forgiveness (like we explored in Chapter 12) is key to overcoming shame.

- **Resentment or Anger Toward Others**
  - Resentment and anger toward others keep us "stuck in the dark," unable to move forward. When we hold on to these emotions, they consume our energy, cloud our perspective, and prevent us from experiencing true freedom. This is why forgiveness is so powerful—not just for others but for our own healing and growth.

To conclude this chapter, we will explore how to step into the light, but first, a deeper discussion on forgiveness feels necessary.

LETTING GO SO WE CAN BE FREE: THE POWER OF FORGIVENESS

A vital part of healing and living a life you desire is learning to let go of what no longer serves you. As previously discussed, forgiveness—both of yourself and others—is essential on this journey of healing. Holding on to bitterness and resentment weighs down the soul, keeping you from experiencing the freedom, joy, and peace that life has to offer.

I want to pause here and share something we later learned about the night Alex's friends brought him to the hospital. His friends had not been honest with us about what happened. We discovered that Alex had taken a pill at a friend's house, and when he slipped into unconsciousness, they did not call 911. We can only assume they were afraid of getting in trouble.

One person came forward and shared that the friend whose house Alex was at had FaceTimed her while Alex lay unconscious and turning blue. The person on FaceTime urged the friend to call 911, but allegedly, the friend refused. Instead, the person present reached out to other friends for help, and they spent close to an hour trying to transport Alex to the hospital themselves.

In an overdose situation, every minute matters. Prompt action is critical, as the effects of fentanyl can often be reversed with naloxone when administered quickly. Additionally, Alex was on his back while he was unconscious, and it's likely his friends didn't know to turn him onto his side. This led to significant aspiration, adding further complications to an already dire situation.

Although Alex's life may have been saved that night had his friends called 911, I do not hold them accountable or blame them for what happened. I have empathy and compassion for them—they were teenagers facing an unimaginably difficult situation. It is also vital to note that Alex made the choice to take the pill that night, so losing his life rests solely in his hands, no one else's. That said, I deeply wish his friends had made a different choice when it came to helping and called 911. At the very least, I wish they had been honest with us about what happened that night.

Forgiveness has been an important part of my grief journey, beginning with self-forgiveness for the ways I fell short in my relationship with Alex and extending that grace to others who fell short. While I've worked to forgive myself—and Alex for the choices he made that night and the last year of his life—the lack of honesty and absence of closure from his friends added another layer of pain.

I chose to forgive all involved. Forgiveness doesn't mean I condone what happened, but I refuse to carry the weight of resentment or the "should haves and could haves" in my heart. Instead, I choose to release those feelings and hold everyone in my heart with love and grace. To withhold forgiveness would be to deny my own worthiness of it. As humans, we all face moments when we need forgiveness and times when we must extend it.

Forgiveness is not about excusing or forgetting someone else's wrongdoings. Instead, it's about releasing their hold over you. It's about letting go of the pain they caused and reclaiming your power. When you forgive, you're not condoning their actions—you're choosing to free yourself from the emotional weight of the past, which is vital to moving forward.

It's also important to understand that forgiveness does not obligate you to continue a relationship with the person who hurt you. Forgiveness can happen entirely in your heart, and if you choose to express it outwardly, you can still set healthy boundaries. These boundaries protect your well-being and ensure that you do not remain in situations that could cause further harm.

This step is deeply personal, and it's essential to assess your unique circumstances to determine what feels right for you. Forgiveness is an act of healing, but it should never come at the cost of your safety or peace. Trust yourself to navigate this process with care, self-compassion, and intention.

When you put forgiveness into practice, you open the door to living fully in the present unburdened by the chains of the past. Forgiveness creates space for healing. It offers a path to renewed peace.

JOURNAL PROMPTS FOR FORGIVING OTHERS

- Acknowledge the pain.
  - Who has hurt you, and how did their actions affect you? What did it take from you? Write about the emotions you feel when you think of this situation.

- **Understand their perspective and separate the act from the person.** Forgiveness is deeply personal, especially when the person you are trying to forgive has caused immense harm. It's important to honor your unique journey and recognize that forgiveness is not a destination or obligation—it's a process that unfolds in your own time and way.
  - Take a moment to reflect on the person's behavior.
    - What might have been motivating their actions? Could they have been acting from their own pain, fear, trauma, or limitations?

IMPORTANT NOTE: This reflection isn't about excusing or justifying their actions, nor does it diminish the pain or trauma you've experienced. Instead, it's about recognizing their humanity—the possibility that their hurtful choices may have been shaped by their own struggles or wounds.

Can you see this person as separate from their actions? It's the distinction between disapproving of what they did and acknowledging that their actions don't define their entire being.

Being sensitive to your own emotions and boundaries is essential here. Some may find it healing to reflect on what may have shaped this person's behavior, such as the person's own pain, circumstances, or limitations. Others may not feel ready or willing to explore this perspective, and that's okay. Forgiveness doesn't require you to understand or empathize with your perpetrator if it feels unsafe or too painful to do so.

Forgiveness doesn't mean forgetting, reconciling, or letting go of accountability. It's about freeing yourself from the weight of resentment or anger so you can heal. If these prompts feel too difficult, skip or modify them to suit your needs. Your healing journey is yours alone, and it's essential to honor where you are and what feels safe for you.

Be gentle with yourself as you explore these prompts. This process is about your growth and peace, and there is no "right" way to navigate it. Trust that, in your own time, you can find a path forward that feels true and brings you peace.

- **Explore the impact.**
  - How has holding onto this hurt or resentment affected your life? Has it impacted your relationships, emotional well-being, or ability to move forward?

- **Reclaim your power.**
  - What would it feel like to let go of this burden? Write about the freedom and lightness you might experience if you no longer carried the weight of this resentment.

- **Affirm your boundaries.** Forgiveness doesn't always mean reconciliation happens. There should be boundaries in place to eliminate further harm.
  - What boundaries do you need to set to protect yourself while still letting go of the pain they caused?

- **Practice gratitude for the lesson.**
  - What has this experience taught you about yourself, others, or life?
  - Even in pain, there are often lessons. Reflect on any growth or understanding that has come from this situation.

- **Release through writing.**
  - If you feel comfortable, write a letter to the person you are forgiving. Express your feelings openly—your hurt, anger, and disappointment—but also state your intention to release the pain and reclaim your peace. You don't need to send this letter; it's for your healing.

- **Visualize forgiveness.**
  - Close your eyes and imagine yourself letting go of this hurt. How does it feel in your body and heart? Write about the emotions and sensations that come with releasing the pain.

- **Commit to letting go.**
  - What steps can you take today to begin forgiving this person or situation? Write a commitment to yourself to release the resentment and reclaim your joy, even if the process feels slow.

Forgiveness is a journey, not a one-time decision, and it is unique to each individual. Allow yourself patience and compassion as you work through this and move toward healing.

STEPPING INTO THE LIGHT AND LIFE-GIVING PRACTICES

Breaking free from darkness begins with conscious action. Regularly evaluate your thoughts and beliefs. Ask yourself: *Is this belief serving me?* If it keeps you stuck in fear, doubt, or pain, it's time to shift your perspective. Growth requires releasing what weighs us down so we can step into a mindset that nourishes and empowers us. The following practices can help you step into the light and cultivate a life of purpose, peace, and growth.

Live in the Present

Mindfulness anchors us in the here and now, where life truly happens. In the present moment, we rediscover beauty in simple things—a breath, a ray of sunlight, the sound of the wind.

Mindful Reflection: Examine your thoughts daily—are they life-giving or draining? Shift toward those that cultivate hope.

Cultivate Gratitude

Gratitude shifts our focus from lack to abundance. You cannot dwell in both at once. By recognizing life's gifts, we reconnect with deeper spaces of faith, love, and hope.

Gratitude practice: Each day, focus on small moments of good.

Speak Life & Seek Support

The words we speak—to ourselves and others—carry immense power. They can either steal, kill, and destroy or inspire, heal, and bring light. Choose words that uplift, empower, and reflect the truth of your worth. Be intentional about the language you use daily, ensuring it fosters growth and wholeness. Equally important is sharing your struggles. Speaking your truth lightens the weight of burdens and brings light into even the darkest places. Vulnerability is courage in action—it opens the door to healing.

Surrender & Trust

Letting go of the need for control invites inner peace. Trusting in a higher power—whether God, the Universe, or something else— allows us to see a bigger picture beyond our immediate struggles.

Shift Your State

Calm your nervous system and create space for clarity through practices like:

- **Breathwork, mindfulness & meditation:** creates inner stillness for clarity and peace.

- **Cold plunges & sauna:** creates a powerful shift in our nervous system state, stimulates circulation, reduces inflammation, and strengthens resilience by exposing the body to temperature extremes.

- **Exercise & movement:** releases stored tension, boosts mood, and strengthens both the body and mind, fostering overall well-being. Physical activity stimulates the release of dopamine and serotonin, the body's natural "feel-good" hormones, which enhance mood, reduce stress, and promote emotional balance.

- **Dance & creative play:** encourages self-expression, joy, and emotional release, allowing you to reconnect with your inner child and freedom.

- **Spending time outdoors:** grounds you in the present moment, offering fresh air, perspective, and a natural reset for the mind and body.

- **Intentional rest:** prioritizing self-care and restoration—they are essential for growth.

Journaling for Growth

Journaling is a powerful tool for self-reflection and transformation. It allows you to uncover limiting beliefs, challenge them, and replace them with empowering truths. Writing down your thoughts creates clarity, helping you recognize patterns that may be keeping you stuck in fear, doubt, or negativity.

Use your journal as a space for gratitude, affirmations, and goal-setting. Reflect on progress, celebrate small wins, and remind yourself of your resilience. Growth happens when we intentionally choose thoughts that uplift and empower us—one word at a time.

Acts of Kindness

Extending kindness to others is a powerful way to bring healing—not just to those you help but to your own soul as well. When we shift our focus outward and offer compassion, generosity, or a simple act of love, we create connection, purpose, and meaning. Kindness has a ripple effect; a small gesture can brighten someone's day, restore hope, and remind both the giver and receiver that they are not alone.

Whether it's a smile, a heartfelt conversation, a helping hand, or an unexpected act of generosity, every act of kindness is a step toward healing—for others and for yourself. In giving, we receive; in lifting others, we rise.

Chapter 16

HUMAN DOING TO HUMAN BEING

As we emerge from the cave, a profound shift in perspective is essential as we move away from merely doing and instead embracing our true nature as a human being.

There's a deeply ingrained message in our society that equates our worth with constant doing: achieving, earning, and proving ourselves through relentless action. We are told that our value lies in what we accomplish, how hard we work, and the things we produce. But this endless cycle of achievement often leads to burnout, discontent, and even physical and mental disease, pulling us further away from our authentic selves.

Living this way dysregulates our nervous system, trapping us in a perpetual state of fight-or-flight, a condition our bodies were never designed to sustain. Stress, often called the silent killer, is a direct consequence of this unsustainable lifestyle.

We've become so consumed with *doing* that we've forgotten how to simply *be*: be present in the moment; be content. We were not designed to be *human doers*, constantly striving, working, and achieving. We were created to experience life fully, to live in the present, and to reconnect with the joy and peace of simply existing. This relentless pursuit pulls us away from our inner truth, disconnects us from our soul, and traps us in the illusions of the outer world. The key to rediscovering our connection to the soul lies in prioritizing being a *human being*.

True living is meant to be soulful, not a constant chase for external validation. Nourishing our soul daily must become a priority, allowing us to reconnect with what truly matters and break free from the exhausting pursuit of worth through doing.

Stillness is vital. Allowing space each day to pause, breathe, and simply *be* is an act of radical self-love. As Dr. Zach Bush so beautifully reminds us, "Are we willing to go to a place where there is no pride because there was nothing to do today, nothing to achieve?" It's okay—essential even—to have days of nothingness, stillness, and simply existing without performing or striving.

You were valuable before you ever accomplished anything, and you remain valuable now. True fulfillment is not found in doing but in *being*. When we reclaim this truth, we move from death to life, from striving to thriving, and from merely existing to truly living.

THE BRIDGE TO LIFE

As you have come to learn throughout these pages, the path to the soul involves shifting our attention from the outer world, where we often seek approval, security, and happiness, toward our inner world, where our true essence resides. The only person you will spend your entire life with is *you,* alongside God. **Love you well. Respect you well.**

Prioritize you well. Soul work is an internal journey that requires us to quiet the distractions of the outside world and turn inward to connect with ourselves and the Divine. It's in this inner space where true healing begins and we can experience the fullness of life.

The journey from wanting to die to choosing life, from battling and overcoming addiction to finding purpose beyond the immense pain of grief and life's difficulties requires leaning on something bigger than ourselves. We must surrender to the Divine, recognizing that we do not walk this path alone. With the Divine by our side, anything is possible. No matter how hopeless or dark life may seem, the bridge to a life of meaning and fulfillment is having a relationship with God (or your higher power). This divine connection helps us move from the illusions of the world to our truth.

Whenever the illusions of the world—fear, lack, and unworthiness—start to take hold, it's essential to turn those feelings over to God. When we feel weary, tired, or uncertain about whether we can continue, we can lean on the Divine to guide us and show us the way forward. The truth is, at times, turning to God has been the only way I have been able to pick myself up and keep moving.

For those who feel like they're at the end of the road and are overwhelmed by despair or hopelessness, the Divine serves as the bridge to wholeness and truth. The key is realizing that this road does not end in darkness but is found when we focus on the light (God's battles). The journey isn't about escaping life; it's about waking up to it. It is about taking our power back from whatever illusions tried to destroy us. It is about seeing the beauty that is all around us, even in the midst of struggle. The problem is, we often walk through life with our eyes closed, or view life through the distorted lens of the world's illusions. It's time to change that lens to one of truth and life-giving words and actions.

LIVING WITH OPEN EYES

The truth is, we get out of life what we claim and the way we choose to see life. Our perception shapes our reality. If we want miracles, we must first claim them. We must shift our perspective to recognize life itself as a miracle.

When we open our eyes, we can see the beauty that surrounds us—whether in the soft hues of a sunrise, the melody of a bird's song, or the quiet stillness of an evening sky. Yet, amid the noise of daily life—the endless doing, striving, and achieving—or repeating of the same patterns that keep us stuck, we often lose sight of these wonders. True living is beautiful when we allow ourselves to truly see it.

Take a moment each day to notice the small miracles around you. Feel the warmth of the sun on your skin, marvel at the intricate patterns of a leaf, or simply breathe deeply and listen to the sounds of the world. These simple acts of presence reconnect us to essential truth: life is precious, *you* are precious, and there is so much to live for.

Never underestimate the healing power of stillness and nature. Time spent among trees, water, mountains, or the open sky can calm the mind, restore the soul, and ground us in the present moment. Nature offers solace to a weary heart, gently reminding us that life continues even in the face of hardship.

Sometimes, peace is found in the simplest moments: sitting quietly in the sun, walking barefoot on the grass, or listening to the wind dance through the trees. These small, intentional acts of presence anchor us in the here and now, helping us reconnect with life's beauty and find peace within ourselves.

When we slow down and open our eyes, we discover that life's beauty has always been there, waiting for us to notice. In these moments of stillness, gratitude, and connection, we find solace, hope, and the strength to keep moving forward.

Chapter 17

THE RIPPLE EFFECT

Everything in life flows from how we see ourselves. By positively shifting our self-perception, we initiate ripples of transformation that touch every aspect of our lives—our confidence, our relationships, our sense of purpose. We begin to attract healthier connections, pursue our passions, and align with the truth of who we are.

This is the power of the ripple effect: **a single shift in perspective spreads outward, shaping our reality and inspiring those around us.** When we recognize ourselves as whole, capable, and worthy, our lives begin to reflect that truth. In doing this, we encourage others to embrace their own worth.

But the impact doesn't stop there. When one person heals, grows, and rises, the effects extend far beyond them—touching their families, communities, and future generations.

THE RIPPLE EFFECT ON RELATIONSHIPS

Connection is essential to our human existence. In fact, I believe a lack of connection, both within ourselves and with others, is at the root of addiction and suicidality. To cultivate meaningful connections, we must first examine our self-perception.

How we see ourselves directly shapes the way we engage with others. If we believe we are unworthy, we may tolerate unhealthy relationships, struggle to set boundaries, or suppress our own needs, leaving us feeling disconnected and alone. But when we recognize our worth, we shift from seeking validation to embodying self-respect. We no longer accept mistreatment and instead cultivate relationships built on love, respect, and mutual support.

A healthy self-perception fosters deeper, more authentic connections, an essential foundation for building a life worth living. When we honor and love ourselves, we teach others how to treat us. By healing our own wounds, we break cycles of dysfunction and model what self-worth looks like. The ripple effect extends beyond us. Our transformation inspires those around us to step into their own healing.

THE RIPPLE EFFECT ON YOUR LIFE'S PURPOSE

How we see ourselves also determines how we show up in the world. If we believe we are insignificant, we may hesitate to pursue our dreams, afraid we have nothing valuable to offer. But when we recognize our own power, we can step boldly into our purpose. We embrace our gifts, take risks, and allow ourselves to be seen.

Each of us has a unique purpose, but doubt and fear can keep us from fully stepping into it. When we shift our mindset from "I am not enough" to "I have something valuable to offer," we unlock our potential. We begin to live with greater intention, seek out opportunities for growth, and share our light with the world, creating that ripple that extends beyond our own journey.

There have been many times in my life when I wanted to play small or stay safe, when fear and doubt crept in. But shrinking myself only made my soul feel lifeless. The more I practice what I preach—stepping into my innate worthiness, releasing the need for approval, and fully owning my gifts—the more alive I become. And the more alive I become, the more I can contribute to others in meaningful ways, which lights my soul on fire.

THE RIPPLE EFFECT ON FAMILIES AND COMMUNITIES

Think about the stories I shared earlier. In each journey of transformation, the impact didn't stop with one person—it extended to everyone around them. A parent overcoming addiction creates a safer, more loving environment for their children. Those children, raised with greater emotional stability, carry that strength into their own lives and relationships. Over time, this ripple can shift the trajectory of an entire family line.

The same is true for communities. When one person finds healing, they inspire those around them. Their courage encourages others to confront their own challenges. Their kindness fosters deeper connection. Their transformation creates space for others to grow. **Communities thrive when the individuals within them are thriving.** One person's journey toward wholeness can ignite collective healing, leading to profound societal shifts.

YOUR TRANSFORMATION HAS A GREATER PURPOSE

This ripple effect reminds us that no change happens in isolation. **Every step you take toward healing, growth, and self-acceptance creates waves that extend far beyond you.** When you choose to rise, you create space for others to rise.

Imagine the impact of one person finding hope after despair, strength after struggle, or love after loss. That transformation touches everyone they encounter, spreading light in ways they may never fully realize. The choice to heal isn't just for ourselves, it's a gift to those we love, those we meet, and generations yet to come.

I have experienced this deeply in my own life as I transformed my pain into purpose and found my way back to a relationship with God. It all began with a single invitation—when my trainer invited me to an Alpha group. That simple act altered the entire course of my grief. Because of it, my daughters now have a relationship with God, and my eleven-year-old was baptized.The impact didn't stop there. Mandy and Randy, whose story I shared earlier, found God through my invitation—just as I did because someone first invited me. Through Him, Randy received the kind of healing only God can provide. Most recently, I invited my administrative assistant to an Alpha group at my church, and she and her son were baptized. The ripple effect is profound—life-giving and life-changing.

By choosing to live with intention, to heal, and to embrace the fullness of life, you have the power to transform not only your own life but also the world around you. **Every act of courage, every moment** of growth, every step of faith, every breakthrough, no matter how small, creates ripples that uplift others.

THE POWER OF YOUR STORY: CREATING RIPPLES OF HOPE

Your pain, grief, and hardships are not without purpose. They have the power to inspire, to heal, and to show others that light exists beyond the cave and that rainbows follow even the darkest storms.

Your life is a miracle. And by embracing this truth, you create ripples of love, healing, and transformation, not only in your life but in the lives of those around you. So ask yourself: **What kind of ripple effect do I want to create?**

Chapter 18

THE SUN ALWAYS RISES AGAIN, AND SO CAN YOU

It is my deepest hope and prayer that, as you reach the final pages of this book, you feel the life stirring within your soul—that you see yourself as a warrior, a miracle, worthy and filled with purpose. As I wrote this last chapter in the British Virgin Islands, holding space for both the weight of the world's darkness and the profound transformations I've witnessed beyond pain, I was reminded of a truth that never fades: hope endures. Always.

As I sat there, I prayed for you, the reader. I prayed that this book would bring hope to the deepest pits of despair and light to the darkest corners of your life. That morning's sunrise was unlike anything I had ever experienced. It was a powerful and undeniable reminder of the beauty, strength, and resilience that each of you carries within.

As the sun began to rise above the horizon, clouds covered the sky. Yet, breathtaking hues of pink and gold broke through the clouds, illuminating the world in a way that felt sacred. At that moment, I heard God whisper to my heart, "There will be cloudy days and storms in life, but the sun is always there—just like the light within you. And even among the clouds there is purpose and beauty."

Life, like the waves of the ocean, brings highs and lows—stormy days and calm waters. But the sun—your inner light—never fades. Even when life feels overwhelming, remember this: the storm is temporary, and your light will shine again, just as the sun rises after the darkest night.

As the sun climbed higher that morning, its rays pierced through the clouds, transforming them into something radiant. It struck me that this is what the world needs from you: your light. No matter how dark the days or how deep the pain, the light you carry is uniquely yours, and the world is brighter when you let it shine. When your light radiates, it not only brightens your own life but also uplifts everyone around you.

SUPPORTING A LOVED ONE THROUGH THE STORM

If you are reading this book as someone supporting a loved one through life's storms, I want you to know how vital your role is. Your presence, compassion, and belief in their ability to rise again are lifelines in their darkest moments.

Supporting someone battling despair, addiction, or the weight of life's challenges can feel overwhelming, but remember, their healing journey is in their hands. Your role is to heal yourself so you can shine a light into their darkness, reminding them that the sun will rise again and that their inner light has not gone out. By doing your own healing and breathing belief into them, you remind them of their inherent worth and their ability to heal.

THE POWER OF LIGHT AFTER DARKNESS

Darkness cannot persist in the presence of light. I encourage you to watch more sunrises to let the beauty of each new day remind you of the light and life within you. The sunrise that morning on the island filled me with an incredible sense of hope and renewal. It reminded me that behind every cloud, behind every storm, the sun is always waiting to shine again.

During that same week on the island, I saw four rainbows—a gentle but profound reminder that beyond the storm, there are rainbows, signifying hope. I want you to see yourself as that rainbow. When life's storms come, remember that you have the strength to emerge on the other side, shining with your own beautiful colors. Rainbows are proof that there is purpose to the pain and that beauty can come from even the darkest moments.

The storms you face are not in vain. They are forging you into a stronger, wiser, more compassionate warrior. Each trial prepares you to step more fully into your purpose, to uncover the gifts within you, and to share those gifts with a world that desperately needs them.

YOU ARE A MIRACLE: STEP INTO YOUR LIFE

In the beginning of this book, we explored the miraculous odds of your existence. That fact alone underscores how significant your life truly is. You are here for a reason, and the world needs you. Any thoughts that try to destroy your sense of worth are lies, illusions designed to keep you from seeing the truth. Your purpose is too great to let life pass by.

If you have been merely existing, allowing life's difficulties to overshadow its beauty, know that this is your moment to rise. The journey you've taken through this book is about uncovering your purpose, letting go of the illusions that have held you back, and stepping into the truth of who you are.

You are already enough, just as you are. Before you accomplish a single thing each day, you are whole. You always have been, and you always will be.

As you move forward, let yesterday's burdens become powerful teachers, propelling you into a new day with a fresh perspective. Approach life with gratitude, remaining open to the miracles that surround you and alive to the possibilities ahead.

To choose life each day and fight for a better tomorrow makes you the ultimate warrior, a soldier in life's most profound battle. You are a Soul Soldier, part of an army of fighters who have faced life's storms and risen stronger.

Your strength, resilience, and choice to rise again create a powerful ripple effect, inspiring others to awaken the warrior within. This is the legacy of a Soul Soldier: choosing life in the face of life's hardest battles, stepping into the light despite the struggles, and paving the way for others to do the same.

The storms you face are shaping you, forging you into a stronger, wiser, and more compassionate warrior. **THIS IS THE RISE OF A SOUL SOLDIER. Welcome to the family.**